LATIN AMERICAN STUDIES

VOLUME 23

Johannes Wilbert, *Editor*

The New Professional in Venezuelan Secondary Education

by

Thomas J. La Belle

With the assistance of

Jan R. Van Orman

Latin American Center
UNIVERSITY OF CALIFORNIA • LOS ANGELES
1973

Copyright © 1973 by the Regents of the University of California
All rights reserved
Library of Congress Catalog Card Number 73-620084
Printed in the United States of America
International Standard Book Number 0-87903-023-2

Preface

This study raises an issue all too often forgotten in terms of the planning of educational reform, including the planning of educational alternatives. That issue concerns the general perceptions held by the teacher, counselor, and administrator in the secondary school. Many educational plans bypass this link in the change process, often assuming that since such individuals are under supervision they will go along with or support the plans made in the ministerial offices. The objective of this study is to explore the attitudes and values of prospective secondary school personnel in terms of professional expectations and orientations, national development priorities, educational goals, and occupational selection and prestige.

The investigation is necessarily exploratory in nature, given the dearth of previous published research on the perception of teachers. Since teachers' salaries often account for more than 80 percent of educational budgets, this lack of prior data is somewhat difficult to comprehend. On the other hand, the training of teachers, with emphasis on subject matter preparation and instructional procedures, has received considerable attention. One assumes, however, that teachers, representing ministerial curricular and instructional policies, do more than transmit intended or deliberate messages to their students. It is felt that they also direct students in occupational and career choice and potentially influence the personal values of those students in unintended or nondeliberate ways. In addition to this link between the Ministry and the student, teachers represent the schooling establishment to parents and other members of the community.

Venezuela is an ideal setting in which to study secondary school personnel. During the sixties there has been a rapid expansion of school facilities in Venezuela and currently a major reform in secondary education is underway. In addition, the advent of the community college coupled with increased demands for middle-level manpower makes the secondary school an extremely important link in the development process. Thus, the perception of the new professional in terms of how schools function in relation to the process of planned change, what role definitions are expected in the administration and decision-making process of schools, and what impact is anticipated by teachers on the lives of their students are important considerations in the context of Venezuela's education and development priorities.

The Latin American Center at the University of California, Los Angeles, through funds granted by the Agency for International Development 211(d) institutional grants program, provided funds for conducting this study. Computer time was received from the UCLA Campus Computing Facility. Questionnaire reproduction plus several weeks of staff assistance for administering the questionnaire throughout Venezuela was supplied by the Venezuelan Ministry of Education and the six institutions participating in the investigation.

The study is an outgrowth of the Latin American Center's current focus on the analysis of educational alternatives in Latin America and was discussed initially in a Graduate School of Education seminar on education in Latin America during the fall quarter of 1970. Several conversations with Venezuelans by the author at a subsequent UCLA seminar on the planning of community colleges in Venezuela resulted in an invitation to pursue the research during the summer of 1971. Lorenzo Monroy, then Director of Secondary and Higher Education for the Venezuelan Ministry of Education, extended the invitation.

Many individuals have assisted in the preparation of this study. I am indebted to Mr. Monroy without whose assistance and direction we would not have been able to pursue the investigation. I am equally indebted to Olga Alberran, also of the Ministry, who aided greatly in the translation of the instrument and accompanied us to the various institutions to administer the questionnaire. I am grateful to the professors and administrators of the six institutions for their cooperation in permitting us to meet with students and to the many individuals who assisted with the administration of the instrument. Finally, I would like to thank Susan Vogeler, of the Venezuelan Ministry of Education, Rafael Revenga, of the Creole Foundation in Caracas, and David O'Shea and James

Wilkie, colleagues at UCLA, for their helpful comments during the preparation of the manuscript.

The most substantial assistance for the completion of the study came from Jan Van Orman, a doctoral student in Comparative and International Education at UCLA. Although technically an assistant, Jan participated more as a colleague. I am especially indebted to him for his contributions in the design of the study and in programming the computer, as well as his assistance with the analysis of the resulting data.

This research was conducted with the financial support of the Agency for International Development. The information and conclusions contained herein do not necessarily reflect the position of A.I.D. or the U.S. Government.

Thomas J. La Belle
UCLA
January 1973

Contents

Tables

Chapter One
Introduction to the Study

In all nations, planning for future growth and development has cast education in an important role. Educational institutions are being asked to train persons for new occupations and to help form compatible "modern" values that will provide both the input and the impetus for expanding and changing the structure of economic and social organization.

Teachers are instrumental in the procedure of implementing new plans and attaining educational aims. Questions concerning the training and selection of teachers and the proper utilization of their skills must be better understood before educational reform can become effective. This study seeks to examine the role of prospective secondary school teachers in the educational process by securing information concerning their attitudes toward education, toward development, and toward the teaching profession.

The worldwide educational revolution of the 1960s had its most dramatic impact on secondary-level schooling.[1] In most societies these schools have been increasingly assigned the task of selecting and certifying individuals and designating social functions (Cicourel and Kitsuse, 1963). This role of servicing other societal institutions has placed the secondary schools in a strategic position within the social system, and has provided these schools with a significant institutional function.

Not only is it the institutional role of the secondary schools but also the nature of their impact upon student career decision-making which makes them important in the achievement of national priorities. It is often during the secondary school age span that students make decisions concerning occupation, higher education, and sociopolitical involvement. Furthermore, graduates

---

[1]Philip H. Coombs, *The World Educational Crisis* (New York: Oxford, 1968); also, *Development of Secondary Education: Trends and Implications,* (Paris: Organization of Economic Cooperation and Development), 1969.

1

of secondary schools are most often those who enter the stream of the middle class where their attitudes and actions will influence the society and economy.[2] Secondary students and graduates represent the active, mobile segment of society.

Of the three primary inputs into the educational system — students, teachers and facilities — teachers are perhaps the most critical because of their relationship to the learning process. Teachers represent the most expensive input of the educational system,[3] and the permanent cadre of the school. Using both collective and personal influence, teachers relate upwardly to the administrative and governmental structures affecting the system.[4] Teachers also interpret national purposes to parents and the community, thus serving as a role model to adults as well as to students.

But it is in the area of directing student learning experiences that teachers are potentially, if not actually, most influential. Teachers not only transmit knowledge but they also structure the learning environment, which places them in the position of orchestrator or intermediary between students and resources.[5]

---

[2] Economic and psychological theories explain the importance of this middle class predisposition to economic and social development. Attitudes of capital formation and consumption are purported to be prerequisite to economic "take off" (see Walt W. Rostow, "The Take-off into Self-sustained Growth," *Economic Journal,* 66 (March 1956) 25-48; David McClelland (*The Achieving Society* [Princeton, N.J.: D. Van Nostrand, 1961]) and John Kunkel (*Society and Economic Growth* [New York: Oxford, 1970]) describe the need for a personal "achievement" orientation in order to sustain progressive growth. Of related significance to this question are the theories of return on educational investment presented primarily by Theodore W. Schultz (see *The Economic Value of Education* [New York: Columbia University Press, 1963]).

[3] Coombs, *The World Educational Crisis*; see also figures in *UNESCO Statistical Yearbook* (Paris: UNESCO, 1970). In Venezuela, 83 percent of the direct operating expenses of the Ministry of Education for 1969 went toward the payment of teachers (*Estadísticas Educacionales,* Departamento de Investigaciones Educacionales, Dirección de Planeamiento, Ministerio de Educación, 1971, Cuadro 8, Página 237).

[4] In many countries, Venezuela included, teachers unions are a potent political force. Not only are governmental policies often influenced by their actions but unions often screen members and control the processes of admission. They also establish professional standards. Two sources of interest to this study are: *Federación Venezolana de Maestros* (Mérida, Venezuela: Universidad de los Andes, 1966); Albert A. Blum, ed., *Teachers Unions and Associations: A Comparative Study* (Urbana, Ill.: University of Illinois Press, 1969).

[5] Such changes are being pushed by rapid innovation in learning concepts and also by the developments within the field of educational technology. See "The Changing Role of the Teacher," *Educational Technology,* 10 (Feb. 1970), entire issue. A more philosophical discussion is Frank Musgrove and Philip H. Taylor, *Society and the Teacher's Role* (London: Routledge & Kegan Paul, 1969).

Teachers come into contact with the majority of the youth of a nation and their ability to adequately socialize and train these children, and facilitate appropriate student decision making, very likely has a profound impact upon the future of individuals as well as upon the nation.

Although the process of forming attitudes during youth has been the subject of much theoretical and some applied social science investigation, relatively little evidence exists which reveals the true role of schooling, and more specifically, teaching, in this socialization process. In attempting to understand the potency of the teacher's position in relation to the child, the scholar may turn to a number of models provided by sociological,[6] psychological,[7] leadership,[8] or political socialization[9] theories. Although very little is known factually about the relationship between teaching and learning, some empirical evidence is now beginning to support intuitive notions that teachers have a significant impact upon the behavior of their students.[10] Admittedly, our state of knowledge as well as our research techniques for studying the phenomena are still quite primitive. The question itself has implications, however, for recruiting, training and utilizing teachers, as well as for expediting the learning process and directing individuals into occupations deemed necessary for socioeconomic growth. For

[6] The contribution of these sciences to this field of thought are diverse and diffuse. See, for example, the theories of social "ascription" of Talcott Parsons, *The Social System* (Glencoe, Ill.: Free Press, 1951).

[7] Educational psychology makes various contributions to this field—see the numerous references on learning theory, role-modeling, personality formation, etc. See, e.g., Georgia Babladelis and Suzanne Adams, *The Shaping of Personality* (Englewood Cliffs, N.J.: Prentice Hall, 1967).

[8] For a specific problematic conceptualization see the "opinion leadership" theory of Llihu Katz and Paul F. Lazarsfeld, *Personal Influence: The Part Played by People in the Flow of Mass Communications* (New York: Free Press, 1955). See also Melvin Seeman, *Social Status and Leadership: The Case of the School Executive* (Columbus, Ohio: Ohio State University, 1960); Wendell Bell, Richard J. Hill, and Charles R. Wright, *Public Leadership* (San Francisco: Chandler, 1961). Many useful theories can be found in the literature on organizational psychology and on management.

[9] A review of this literature, and the conceptualization of a theory (also relating to "occupational socialization") to a research problem is contained in David R. Evans *Teachers as Agents of National Development: A Case Study of Uganda* (New York: Praeger Special Studies, 1971).

[10] *Do Teachers Make a Difference? A Report on Recent Research on Pupil Achievement,* (Washington, U.S. Office of Education, 1970); Ned A. Flanders, *Teacher Influence, Pupil Attitudes, and Achievement* (Washington: U.S. Office of Education, 1965).

these reasons, studies of the attitudes and predispositions of prospective secondary school personnel seem warranted.

In Venezuela, planning for national development has led to innovative educational reform proposals, many of which are now being prepared for implementation. Hansen (1970), for example, reports the recent plan for national school decentralization, and in February of 1971 a public law was signed creating ten post-secondary technical training institutes (colegios universitarios) — thus introducing a new level of schooling and new educational opportunities. These plans and others accentuate the need for a brief overview of the educational process and system in Venezuela.

A. Education in Venezuela

The Venezuelan constitution sets the foundation for free and compulsory education for all citizens seven to fourteen years of age. The government school system consists of three phases: (1) preprimary and primary education; (2) secondary, academic, technical, and normal (primary school teacher training) school education; and (3) university-level education. Privately sponsored education, both ecclesiastic and secular, exists at all levels and enrolls approximately 15 percent of the students (*Más y Mejor Educación;* 1970).

The administrative structure of the education system is, for the most part, centralized under a minister of education appointed by the president of the nation. Municipalities and states also control some of the educational institutions, with special emphasis at the primary level. Public universities operate under the principle of autonomy and are organized by a special counsel of university representatives. Additionally, there are some primary, secondary, and specialized schools that are governed by government ministries other than education. The Ministry of Education, however, controls and authorizes curricula and educational standards for all educational institutions, public or private, with the exception of universities. The annual governmental expenditures for the educational system totals approximately 22 percent of the national budget (*Memoria y Cuenta*, Vol. II, 1971).

Two periods in recent Venezuelan history are characterized by their deleterious effects on the educational system. These periods include the years 1910-1935 when the dictator Juan Vicente

4

Gómez was Venezuela's president, and the years 1948-1958 when Marcos Pérez Jiménez, also a dictator, was in power. Under both dictatorial leaders, the formal school system declined in number of schools, students, and teachers. For example, in 1886 there were 1,957 primary schools whereas in 1935 there were only 1,432. The year 1935 found only 20 percent of the school-age population in school and 80 percent illiteracy among the total populace. At the secondary level, the situation was little better. In 1889 there were thirty-six secondary schools in Venezuela while in 1934 there were forty, of which half were privately sponsored, and all were staffed by about 200 part-time teachers (Sánchez, 1963).

Between 1935 and 1948, the educational system expanded greatly. When Pérez Jiménez became influential, however, first under a military junta (1948-1952), and subsequently on his own (1952-1958), the number of public schools, teachers, and students declined once again while private schools flourished. Enrollment, for example, at the National Pedagogic Institute of Caracas, founded in 1942, was 611 students in 1949-1950, and 322 students in 1956-1957 (Sánchez, 1963).

The universities came under special attack during the Pérez Jiménez period. Central University in Caracas, founded in 1725 as the Royal and Pontifical University of Caracas, was closed during the 1951-52 academic year. Two private universities in Caracas, Catholic Andrés Bello University and Santa María University, both founded in 1953, begun out of necessity as a result of the political constraints. These two private universities joined the already existing University of the Andes at Mérida (1810) and the reopened University of Zulia at Maracaibo (1947).

> After the national universities were granted autonomy in 1958 and with the reappearance of political parties as consequence of the rebirth of democratic life, the public universities were turned into political battlegrounds. In other words, their own internal self-governing process was intervened and mediatized by political parties that vied for power and prestige. Our universities have a long standing history going back to the 1920's of fighting oppressive political regimes. This precedent was exercised once more at the end of 1957 and the first months of 1958 when the universities presented a united front to restaurate and defend democracy. (Revenga, 1970:29).

In 1958, when Rómulo Betancourt and his Acción Democrática party assumed national leadership, a renewed emphasis was placed on expanding educational facilities and opportunities. In 1958, for example, there were 3,850 secondary schoolteachers with only a third of them having received formal training (Revenga, 1971), whereas by 1970-71, of the 11,626 Venezuelan trained secondary schoolteachers, approximately 60 percent were graduates of post-secondary universities (licenciados or doctores) and pedagogic institutes (*Memoria y Cuenta*, Vol. II, 1971). The period from 1958 to 1971 also saw secondary school enrollment expand from 70,000 to 498,346 (*Más y Mejor Educación*, 1970; *Memoria y Cuenta*, Vol. II, 1971), and the opening of the University of Carabobo at Valencia (1958), the University of Oriente at Cumaná (1959), the Experimental Pedagogic Institute at Barquisimeto (1959), Simón Bolívar University at Caracas (formerly the University of Caracas) (1970), and Metropolitan University (1970), also at Caracas. In addition, the Universidad de la Región Centro Occidental and the Politécnico Superior, both located in Barquisimeto, were founded during this period.

Administrative and organizational changes also occurred between 1958 and 1971. At the time of this writing, the administration of schools is being decentralized into eight regions (Hansen, 1970), while organizationally there exists an emphasis on preprimary education and postsecondary technical institutes[11] and community colleges. In addition, the secondary school is undergoing considerable alteration with the institution of a three-year first cycle providing a common, general education for all students, followed by a diversified, two-year second cycle at which time students specialize in either normal, technical-vocational, or academic secondary subject matter fields.

Teacher training, however, with the exception of new in-service programs and the addition of facilities, has remained organiza-tionally and administratively much the same. Teachers are trained for primary instruction in normal schools (secondary school equivalent) while personnel are trained for the secondary level at either universities or the two pedagogic institutes. The primary responsibility for secondary school teacher training traditionally rests with the two pedagogic institutes while universities also train

---

[11] The first such institute, the Instituto Universitario de Tecnologia, designed for the preparation of middle level technicians, is in operation in Caracas (*Memoria y Cuenta, Tomo I* [1971]).

secondary level teachers as well as specialists in administration, counseling, and evaluation.[12] During the 1967-68 academic year, there were 4,456 individuals preparing for secondary school employment. The enrollment was distributed as follows: Central University, 884; University of the Andes, 537; University of Zulia, 1,752; University of Carabobo, 847; University of Oriente, 83; Andrés Bello University, 353; and the two pedagogic institutes, 3,380 (*Más y Mejor Educación*, 1969).

Entrance requirements differ somewhat between the universities and the pedagogic institutes. The schools of education at the universities require that the applicant have either a secondary school diploma in the sciences or the humanities, or that he be certified as a primary education teacher and have completed at least three years of professional experience. The universities award the title of licenciado to those students who complete the university's four-year curriculum and who possess an academic secondary school diploma.

Entrance to one of the two pedagogic institutes requires a diploma from any secondary school, including normal and technical-commercial institutions. The largest percentage of first-year students at the two institutes, however, tends to be academic secondary school graduates. For example, between 1964 and 1968, the Pedagogic Institute at Caracas enrolled 1,802 academic secondary, 1,604 normal, and 77 technical-commercial school graduates as first-year students.[13]

The pedagogic institutes, as well as the universities, provide a four-year course of study including both subject matter specialization and teacher or other professional preparation designed to train secondary school personnel. Currently, the programs at both types of institutions proceed from a general education in the arts and sciences common to all majors, to an emphasis on specialized subject matter, professional preparation and, if appropriate, practice teaching for those planning to become teachers. The

[12]The Ministry has also proposed that university graduates be certified as secondary teachers in their fields of competence after completing a short course in order to prevent the forecast deficit of secondary teachers (Rafael Revenga, personal communication, November 1972).

[13]*Matrícula del Instituto Pedagógico de Caracas Discriminada por Entidades Federales y Otras Nacionalidades, El Pedagógico en Cifras*, Boletin del Servicio de Estadística no. 4, Año Lectivo, 1967-68 (Caracas: Pedagogic Institute, n.d.).

Pedagogic Institute at Caracas is organized around the following subject matter departments: biology and chemistry; Spanish, literature, and Latin; physical education; geography and history; modern languages; mathematics and physics; and pedagogy. The Pedagogic Institute at Barquisimeto consists of the departments of literature and modern languages; mathematics; experimental sciences; social sciences; and technical education. The following list reports the number and major of teachers graduated from the two pedagogic institutes during 1968.[14]

Pedagogic Institute, Caracas

Major	Number of graduates
Biology and chemistry	78
Spanish, literature, Latin	44
Physical education	18
French	20
Geography and history	52
Modern languages	19
Mathematics and physics	17
	248

Pedagogic Institute, Barquisimeto

Major	Number of graduates
English and Spanish	13
Mathematics	10
Mathematics and physics	1
Spanish and literature	13
Chemistry	12
Biology	14
Biology and chemistry	2
History	10
Geography	3
History and Geography	2
Chemistry and physics	1
Industrial arts	1
	82

[14]*Ibid. Instituto Pedagógico Experimental, Informe Anual*—1968-69, Barquisimeto, Julio de 1969 (Barquisimeto: Pedagogic Institute, n.d.).

Given the rather erratic development of education in Venezuela, caused principally by the neglect of the system by the two dictatorial governments, the decade of the sixties saw an enormous expansion of facilities along with a concomitant growth in numbers of enrolled students. In 1970-71 the educational system at all levels enrolled 2,567,433 students, or 24.7 percent of the total population. With this quantitative expansion, however, other educational issues and problems with which Venezuelan educators are concerned have emerged. Dropout and failure rates, for example, are high. In 1968-69 approximately one-third of those who entered primary school six years before completed the six years and less than 50 percent of the population under twenty-four years of age were registered in school (Revenga, 1969).

B. Occupational Choice

Basically such educational statistics emanate from, and are intertwined with, social and economic conditions existing in the nation as a whole. The population of Venezuela, for example, is growing at a rate of 3.6 percent per year, 54 percent of that population is less than nineteen years of age, and about 65 percent of the approximately 11 million inhabitants live in urban areas (Revenga, 1969). Although the economy is expanding at a rapid rate, the creation of new jobs, especially in the areas of agriculture, hydrocarbons and mines, manufacturing, construction, and energy resources must take place in order to meet the demand by young persons for employment opportunities as well as continued economic growth for the nation. Although jobs in these several sectors currently exist, the demand is for skilled, as well as trained middle level, manpower which currently is in relatively short supply. For example, it was estimated that in 1970, about 80 percent of the 207,000 persons who reached their eighteenth birthday had no more than six years of schooling (Revenga, 1969). In addition, of those students enrolled at the secondary school level during 1968-69, approximately 64 percent were in academic secondary schools specializing in humanities or one of the sciences (*Más y Mejor Educación*, 1970).

One of the most urgent dilemmas for educational planners is that of attracting and directing qualified individuals to fulfill needed positions in the labor force. Competing opportunities

9

often lure the quality graduates to particular sectors of the economy, most often toward prestige fields, creating oversupply in some areas and critical shortages in others. Schools serve as one mechanism of social differentiation and may provide some understanding of the diverse forces that impinge upon occupational choice.

Gordon Ruscoe (1968) has conducted a preliminary investigation into this phenomena by isolating some variables that influence the occupational preferences of secondary school students in Venezuela. He reports that more students in his sample (97 percent) aspired to professional than to other positions within society – an unrealistic and impractical goal. He further indicated that teachers seem to be the least important of nine factors identified as influencing students in making their occupational choices. Ruscoe does conclude, however, that there are groups of students who are susceptible to the influences that are located within the schooling process and that these students ". . . might profit considerably from assistance and guidance at the secondary school level." In studying the influence of teachers on performance aspirations of students, Rosenfeld and Zander (1961) found that teachers do facilitate realistic decision making on the part of some students. Evans (1971) has also indicated the potentially viable role for the school in the "occupational socialization" of students. These studies are anything but conclusive, however, and very little sophisticated work has been done relating teachers to such phenomena of social development.[15]

The processes by which a population becomes distributed within the occupational structure of society has been the topic of considerable inquiry by sociologists and educators.[16] Further

[15] Very little empirical research with broad inferential value exists; most studies relating teachers to social change have been purely statistical description. For examples refer to UNESCO and to the excellent recent national studies on teachers by the Organization of Economic Cooperation and Development (OECD). See also "Teachers in American Society," in Charles B. Nam and John K. Folger, *Education of the American Populations* (Washington, D.C.: U.S. Bureau of the Census, 1967). By far the most valuable analytical studies on this question are those done by Orlando Albornoz, *El Maestro y la Educación en la Sociedad Venezolana* (Caracas, 1965), and Robert J. Havighurst and Aparecida J. Gouveia, *Brazilian Secondary Education and Socio-Economic Development* (New York: Praeger, 1969). Gouveia has elaborated on the basic material presented in the joint 1969 report in A. Solari and S. M. Lipset, *Elites in Latin America* (New York: Oxford, 1967) and elsewhere.

[16] See, e.g., a collection of reports in Amitai Etzioni, ed., *The Semi-Professions and Their Organization* (New York: Free Press, 1969).

10

understanding concerning this phenomenon is likely to have implications for the role of the school, and the teacher, in influencing individual decision making.[17] The issue is complex, however, and further inquiry demands some refinement of the question.

One case lending itself to more explicit investigation is that of the choice by students to enter the teaching profession, and to remain in teaching.[18] The re-entry of these graduates back into the school system, and consequently into the position of directing the same schooling experience for others, would make the attitudes of teachers particularly important in the socialization process in the school. Thus, aspiring teachers are a unique population relating to the question of occupational choice if we regard the school to be an environment facilitative of such decision making.

It is a basic tenet of this inquiry that certain attitudes predispose individuals toward various courses of action (Jahoda and Warren, 1966) and that attitudes are differentially formed (Parsons, 1949). These assumptions lead to the conclusion that differences in the attitudes of teachers will have implications for the future behavior of teachers and perhaps for the influence that teachers have upon the attitudes, values, and behavior of students.[19] Also, an understanding of the socialization processes within the teaching profession, and factors that encourage or inhibit one's performance of his teaching duties, and his very choice to remain, or not, in teaching, will permit planners to more accurately predict the future and the character of the nation's cohort of teachers.

[17]For a reference work on this role see the compilation by A. Morrison and D. McIntyre, *Teachers and Teaching* (Baltimore, Md.: Penguin, 1969); also B. Othaniel Smith, *Research in Teacher Education* (Englewood Cliffs, N.J.: Prentice-Hall, 1971).

[18]A number of important studies have been conducted relating the occupational prestige and status of teaching; this work seems to have some influence upon teacher retention and satisfaction. See G. Bernbaum et al., "Intra-Occupational Prestige Differentiation in Teaching," and Eric Hoyle, "Professional Stratification and Anomie in the Teaching Profession," both in *Pedagógica Europaea* (London: W. & R. Chambers, 1969). See also the summary, *Survey of the Status of the Teaching Profession in the Americas* by Margarita Davies (Washington, D.C.: World Confederation of Organizations of the Teaching Profession, 1964).

[19]The assumption posited here is also the thesis of David Evans (Teachers as Agents of National Development: A Case Study of Uganda) whose study served as a prototype for this investigation.

C. Areas of Inquiry

Several major issues and questions emerge as the focuses of the current investigation. First, both the paucity and the poverty of existing research on teachers dictate the need for a descriptive and demographic investigation of the individuals who make up the prospective population of secondary school personnel. Information of this sort is important in that it provides a basis for assessing trends in major fields of study, institutional affiliation, and personal, family, and educational background factors. Thus, the first area of inquiry is designed to describe the population sampled and to interrelate such descriptors in an attempt to identify those students who are preparing to enter the education profession.

The second major question that needed to be asked by those concerned with the teaching force related to employment aspirations and expectations. The importance of these areas relates to the intentions of students to pursue the career for which they are being prepared, their commitment to the profession, and their preferences for subjects that they wish to teach, as well as their preference for the type and locale of the secondary school where they anticipate being placed. In addition, issues concerning membership in teachers' unions, involvement with the administration of the school, and the importance of religious instruction are included.

The third major question relates to the perception of prospective secondary school personnel with respect to Venezuela's educational needs and development priorities. Here, the inquiry is aimed at securing attitudinal information relating to reform, both quantitatively and qualitatively, in the educational system, as well as information relating to the more general needs and priorities of national development in Venezuela.

A fourth area of inquiry concerns the student's perception of the purposes of education, the role of the school in relation to society, school management and decision making, and the question of who has the responsibility for student learning.

A final area relates to why people become teachers, what factors and people influence this decision, and what the role of the teacher is in guiding others in occupational decision making. Equally significant in this regard is the perception of prospective secondary school personnel of the prestige of their own and other

12

occupations, the occupational needs of Venezuela, and the values that have guided the students' selection for their particular job preferences.

The need for studying secondary school personnel, both during their preparation as well as in the field, is a first step in assessing the actual and potential impact that such individuals have on their students' personal needs and national orientations. As enrollment continues to increase at all levels of the educational system, this need for research becomes increasingly important. It is anticipated, for example, that in the year 2000, approximately 1.5 million students will be enrolled at the secondary level, and 15,899 prospective secondary school personnel will be enrolled at the pedagogic institutes, a six-fold increase in less than thirty years.

D. Research Methods

Approximately one academic year (1970-71) was spent in reviewing the relevant research on teachers, developing a rationale for the investigation, and preparing the questionnaire (Appendix S) for securing the necessary information from Venezuelan students. Five major areas were included in the final questionnaire: (1) demographic characteristics; (2) professional expectations and orientations; (3) educational needs and development priorities; (4) attitudes toward education; and (5) occupational selection, prestige, and values.

The survey questionnaire employed in this study was developed from a variety of related instruments. During the winter and spring of 1971 survey instruments utilized in studies by Havighurst (Brazilian secondary schools), Evans (teachers in Uganda), Ruscoe (Venezuelan students occupational aspirations), Educational Testing Service (Princeton, N.J., "College Student Questionnaire"), along with other work that was subsequently rejected, were scrutinized in relation to the purposes of this inquiry. Following three revisions, each of which was reviewed by a pool of interested colleagues, a final English version of the questionnaire was reduced from the 600 original questionnaire items to the present 130 questions representing 189 types of information.

13

The English version of the questionnaire was translated into Spanish by Venezuelan students enrolled at UCLA, and the translation was subsequently reviewed and corrected in a second version prepared with the assistance of officials of the Venezuelan Ministry of Education. The final version was pretested on a small group of students in Caracas and, following minor revisions, reproduced for this study by staff members of the Ministry of Education.

In the original research strategy it had been planned to include only the two pedagogic institutes in the sample, the Instituto Pedagógico de Caracas and the Instituto Pedagógico Experimental de Barquisimeto, the principal trainers of secondary level educators in Venezuela. It was presumed these institutions would provide a representative cross section of subjects for this inquiry. Contacts with several other universities in Venezuela generated considerable interest in the study, however, and provided an unexpected advantage. It is well known that admission to higher-level institutions is both geographically and socially selective, especially in Latin America. Also, the universities in Venezuela definitely display different educational and activity environments which, if they do not serve to influence individuals differently, at least confer upon their graduates varying social reputations. In other words, students either by selection or by indoctrination, are not randomly distributed among the institutions of higher education.

We are interested here principally in the typical student preparing for a secondary school career. Selective differences within the credentialing system (the universities) may begin to explain the distribution of the target population being studied. A sample of comparable respondents drawn from outside the pedagogic institutes may permit a greater clarification of the influence of external systemic selective factors on this population. While the two pedagógicos are of principal interest to the subject, the other major universities with schools of education permit a sample comparison. Most importantly, the four additional institutions that participated in this study provided an intersample comparison to test the randomness and representativeness of the respondent group.

The limited resources available for the study necessitated the survey format with self-report questionnaires. Administration of the instrument had to be conducted among intact classrooms of students; consequently the sampling stratification was done only in the two pedagogic schools where there were numerous classrooms from which to choose. As a result, the cohort measured in the nonpedagogic schools is not stratified. In the pedagógicos care was taken to select groupings of students who represented each of the year-in-school and subject major categories.[20]

The questionnarie was administered in July of 1971 just before the close of the school year.[21] Respondents completed the survey in intact classroom groupings; the presence of test administrators was minimized in an attempt to avoid associating the study with individuals who might precipitate distorted reactions to the questionnaire. Respondent anonymity was assured; the questionnaire required less than an hour to complete.

The questionnaires were returned to the UCLA campus for processing and analysis. All data were interpreted and coded by the two investigators and transcribed to computer cards. Three principal computations were made of the data at the computing facility at UCLA. In the first analysis routine data screening provided descriptions and summaries of the total respondent groups. In the second analysis cross-tabulation procedures were employed to prepare summaries of item responses by subgroup categories. These subgroup profiles permitted interdata comparisons by institution and respondent's sex, age, year-in-school, major subject, and level of parents' education. The Statistical Package for the Social Sciences (SPSS) computer programs were utilized for these two analyses. Finally, a multivariate analysis of variance of the responses to the fifty-three "agree-disagree" attitude items provided tests of statistical significance for each of the respondent subgroup categories mentioned above. Univariate scores identified significantly different response patterns between respondent subgroups.[22]

[20]Professor Alejandro Togorres and his staff are to be thanked for their assistance in drawing the sample and administering the questionnaire at the Instituto Pedagógico de Caracas.

[21]Student revolts had closed the schools just before this survey (indeed, the final sample from the Universidad Central de Venezuela was gathered only hours before a major riot on campus which led to the deposition of the rector).

[22]In addition to the data processed to present the descriptive results reported here, the fifty-three attitude items that were subjected to statistical analysis (MANOVA) were further analyzed as to their heterogeneity in separate factor analyses (see Appendix T).

15

While the data analyses supply detailed comparisons between respondent subgroups, and in some cases provocative results, the reader should be cautioned not to generalize subgroup differences. Comparative analyses merely served the end of scientific exploration and facilitated our purpose of raising pertinent questions for educational policy planners. The lack of a random sample makes it unwise to imply the representativeness of any subgroup designees. The patterns and trends that did emerge were taken, however, to provide an accurate representation of the background, views, and attitudes of the *total* population of prospective Venezuelan secondary school personnel.

Analyses of the data did provide some confidence in the results and the procedures used. It should be recognized that as a "descriptive" report this study has not undertaken extensive explanation of these data. This monograph has not attempted to go beyond the data themselves except to raise pertinent research questions. It is an empirical study and a first attempt to investigate a particular population in Venezuela.

Chapter Two
The Sample

This chapter reports the background descriptive data of the sample population, and includes sections devoted to institutional, personal, family, employment, and secondary school characteristics of the students sampled.

All demographic data were analyzed for the total sample and by making subgroup comparisons for six variables that are referred to throughout the report: institution, sex, age, major, year-in-school, and level of parental[1] education. It was expected that the principal variation among subgroups would be found within these categories. A cross-tabulation computer program[2] was used enabling within-subgroup comparisons to be made for every survey item. The discussion that follows is, therefore, directed toward describing and analyzing the sample in terms that describe respondent educational and personal backgrounds; total sample and subgroup descriptions are made.

The sample comprised 638 students majoring in education who were attending institutions during the month of July 1971. A self-report questionnaire with 189 response items was administered to available intact classrooms representing select year and subject matter groupings. The questionnaire required both open-ended and multiple-choice responses. An attempt was made to sample the attitudes of students from administrative, counseling, evaluation, and teaching subject matter specializations at various stages in their university careers.

---

[1] Father's education level was used to measure this variable.

[2] SPSS "Crosstabs;" run at the UCLA Campus Computing Facility.

I. Institutional Background (Appendix A)

A. Institution Affiliation (Questions 130, 115, 116)

Students from six Venezuelan institutions of higher education studying for baccalaureate degrees in the field of education were administered questionnaires.[3] The sample was composed of education students from four major universities and from the two pedagogic institutes in Venezuela. The institutions, representing differing geographical areas of the country, were the Instituto Pedagógico at Caracas, the Instituto Pedagógico Experimental at Barquisimeto, the Universidad Central de Venezuela at Caracas, the Universidad Católica Andrés Bello at Caracas, the Universidad del Oriente at Cumaná, and the Universidad de Los Andes at San Cristóbal.

1) *Enrollment.* The majority of the sample was drawn from the two pedagogic institutes which are the principal trainers of secondary level educators in Venezuela. Of the total sample, 39 percent were enrolled in the Pedagógico at Caracas and 33 percent were enrolled in the Pedagógico at Barquisimeto. Central University and the University of the Andes accounted for 12 percent and 11 percent, respectively, of the sample, while Oriente and Andrés Bello Universities supplied a total of 5 percent of the sample (table 1).

2) *Year-in-school.* Students were sampled from each of the four school years: 24 percent were first-year students, 32 percent were second-year students, 15 percent were third-year students, and 29 percent were fourth-year students.

Virtually all of the first-year students sampled were from the two pedagogic institutes (table 1). Seventy percent of second-year students were drawn from the Pedagogic Institute of Caracas, the third-year sample came primarily from Central University and the University of the Andes, and the fourth-year sample came from the pedagogic institutes, the University of the Andes, and Catholic

---

[3] Since the sample is not representative of the various education faculties in the six institutions, reference to particular institutional comparisons should be treated as exploratory leading to the further development of hypotheses for research.

TABLE 1

Number of Students by Institution and Year in School[a]

Institution	Year in School				Total
	1	2	3	4[b]	
Catholic University Andrés Bello	0	0	0	21	21 (3.4%)
Central University	1	29	41	3	74 (12.1%)
Pedagogic Institute, Caracas	56	137	12	38	243 (39.6%)
Pedagogic Institute, Barquisimeto	90	27	2	74	193 (31.4%)
Los Andes University	1	3	28	36	68 (11.1%)
University of the Oriente	1	0	8	6	15 (2.4%)
Total	149	196	91	178	614
	(24.3%)	(31.9%)	(14.8%)	(29.0%)	(100%)

[a]In the tables and text, note that owing to varying response patterns the total number of students answering any one question differs.

[b]Including 1% "fifth"-year students. Some students indicated they were enrolled in their fifth year (1% of the total sample, 8 persons). As there was no fifth academic year recognized by any of these institutions, it is presumed that these students are holdovers from the fourth year.

University Andrés Bello. This uneven distribution of respondent year-in-school stratification resulted from sampling restrictions and not from design.

3) *Major.* The sample may be divided into two broad specialization categories: administrators (administration, counseling, evaluation) and teachers (subject matter specialists). The subject matter majors came almost exclusively from the two pedagogic institutes. Humanities, natural science, technical-vocational, and commercial plus other nonclassifiable majors predominated at the Pedagogic Institute at Barquisimeto, whereas language, physical science, and physical education majors were drawn more from the Pedagogic Institute at Caracas. More than half of the pedagogy (education philosophy and theory) majors were drawn from Central University while a somewhat higher percentage of counseling-evaluation-administration majors were from the University of the Andes (table 2).

19

TABLE 2

Number of Students by Major and Institution

Major	Institution							Total
	Andrés Bello University	Central University	Pedagogic Institute, Caracas	Pedagogic Institute, Barquisimeto	Los Andes University	University of the Oriente		
Pedagogy	19	50	10	1	2	1		83 (13.8%)
Counseling, administration, evaluation	1	23	1	0	62	0		87 (14.5%)
Humanities	0	0	37	57	0	0		94 (15.6%)
Language	0	0	50	18	0	3		71 (11.8%)
Physical science	1	0	96	9	0	4		110 (18.3%)
Natural science	0	0	23	76	0	3		102 (17.0%)
Technical-Vocational	0	1	2	7	0	1		11 (1.8%)
Physical education	0	0	17	1	0	0		18 (3.0%)
Commerce and others	0	0	4	19	0	2		25 (4.2%)
Total	21 (3.5%)	74 (12.3%)	240 (39.9%)	188 (31.3%)	64 (10.6%)	14 (2.3%)		601 (100%)

B. Major Field of Study (Question 117)

1) *Enrollment.* Specializations in pedagogy and counseling-evaluation-administration were offered only in Central, Andrés Bello, and Los Andes Universities. The sample was distributed by major field of study as follows: physical science (18 percent), natural science (17 percent), humanities (15 percent), counseling-evaluation-administration (15 percent), pedagogy (14 percent), languages (12 percent), commercial and "other" majors (4 percent), physical education (3 percent), and technical-vocational education (2 percent). As noted, these respondents were not drawn in equal proportions from the institutions surveyed; rather, enrollments by major field of study were constrained by the institution and year-in-school distributions mentioned.

2) *Year-in-school.* When the sample is stratified by major and year in school, several observations are appropriate. Students majoring in pedagogy and counseling-evaluation-administration (enrollees of Central, Andrés Bello, and Los Andes universities) were present in the second-, third-, and fourth-year cohorts, but this group constituted the entire third-year sample. The first-year student sample included students only from four major fields: humanities, languages, natural sciences, and commercial and "other" majors. The second- and fourth-year student subgroups are the most representative: the distribution in the second-year cohort included all majors and the fourth-year cohort included all but humanities, physical education, and commercial majors.

3) *Parental education.* The educational background of the parents of students sampled reflected a heavy predominance of students whose parents had a primary school education or less (74 percent). Of the thirty-seven students who reported having parents with a postsecondary education, approximately 25 percent were pedagogy majors and 25 percent were language majors. Of all the pedagogy and language majors, however, students whose parents had a postsecondary education accounted for only about 15 percent of the total of each of the respective fields. Forty-six percent of the technical-vocational majors reported having parents without any formal education which contrasted with 14 percent of the

21

total student sample who reported having parents with no formal education (table 3), suggesting that technical-vocational majors exhibit the greatest upward mobility in terms of formal education.

C. Practice Teaching (Question 118)

An attempt to assess the impact that practice teaching might have on the attitudes of education students led us to inquire as to the number of students who had in fact completed their practice teaching. Although practice teaching has not been analyzed as an independent variable in this report, it is important to note that about 32 percent of the sample had practice teaching experience. Of those who had practice taught, 44 percent were enrolled in the Pedagogic Institute at Barquisimeto and approximately 19 percent each were enrolled in the Pedagogic Institute at Caracas and the University of the Andes. Since 85 percent of those who indicated that they had practice taught were in their fourth year in school, it was to be expected that these students would respond differently to attitudinal items on the basis of age and experience differences. As shown later in this report, differentiation by year-in-school did appear with some frequency in relation to the attitudinal items included in the questionnaire.

II. Personal Background (Appendix B)

A. Sex (Question 119)

The total sample was comprised of 59 percent females and 41 percent males. This ratio of men to women was generally the same across all institutions sampled.[4]

1) *Age.* There was a higher percentage of females among younger age students (89 percent of 17-18 year olds) and a higher

---

[4]Some frequency variations do occur within subgroupings of respondents as they are compared by institution, sex, age, major, and other demographic-descriptive characteristics. These variations appear primarily within particular, and usually less important subsamples (e.g., the sample drawn from Oriente University contained 77 percent male respondents; however, this percentage represents only 15 students or a total of 2 percent of the total respondents in the study. Consequently, such variations will not be reported except as they have special importance for qualifying results which are reported in this study.)

TABLE 3

Number of Students by Major and Parental Education

Major	Level of Parental Education								Row Total
	No Formal Schooling	Some Primary Education	Graduate Primary School	Some Secondary Education	Graduate Secondary School	Some University Education	Graduate University	Post-University Education	
Pedagogy	8	25	16	17	3	6	2	2	79 (13.8%)
Counseling, administration, evaluation	15	31	22	11	3	0	1	1	84 (14.7%)
Humanities	11	35	25	11	4	0	2	3	91 (15.9%)
Languages	7	18	24	8	5	1	8	0	71 (12.4%)
Physical science	15	32	22	14	7	4	1	0	95 (16.6%)
Natural science	11	36	28	14	7	2	0	1	99 (17.3%)
Technical-Vocational	5	2	3	0	0	0	0	1	11 (1.9%)
Physical education	2	6	5	2	1	2	0	0	18 (3.1%)
Commerce and other	4	10	5	4	2	0	0	0	25 (4.4%)
Total	78 (13.6%)	195 (34%)	150 (26.2%)	81 (14.1%)	32 (5.6%)	15 (2.6%)	14 (2.4%)	8 (1.4%)	573 (100%)

percentage of males among older students (60 percent of students age 25 and older) (table 4). The predominance of men among students may indicate a stronger likelihood for males to return for teacher training after pursuing other educational or job alternatives. Women seem less likely to be pursuing university degrees in education as they become older, a reflection, perhaps, of limited freedom or opportunity for women to return to school after employment or marriage. Also, the female majority among younger students may be influenced by the more recent popularization of secondary teaching as a career opportunity for women. This age-sex relationship was also observed in the sample distribution by school class; males constituted a larger percentage of the sample as year-in-school increased.

2) *Major.* There was some bias in the distribution of the sample by sex when subdivided by subject specialization or major. Physical science, technical-vocational, and physical education specializations reflected heavy enrollment by males while pedagogy, counseling, humanities, languages, natural science, and commerce and other nonclassified specializations were dominated by females.

3) *Parental education.* Although the educational background of the parents of the total sample was generally low, variation was observed between the education level of parents controlled by the sex of students. Table 5 demonstrates that a higher percentage of male students had parents with no formal education while females more frequently had parents who had a primary and secondary education; females constituted 77 percent of the sample for those students whose parents had completed secondary education.

This trend suggests that the educational attainment among males, when compared with females, may be considerably higher. In other words, because males preparing for careers in secondary education are morelikely to come from homes where the educational level of the parents is low they are registering greater educational mobility than females.

In his study of secondary teachers in Brazil, Havighurst reported that persons from a relatively high socioeconomic background who were found in the teaching profession were almost exclusively women. There seemed to be a social role perception that

TABLE 4

Number of Students by Sex and Age

Sex	Years of Age									Total
	17-18	19-20	21-22	23-24	25-26	27-28	29-30	31-35	36 and Over	
Male	3	13	50	51	41	22	20	24	17	241 (40.9%)
Female	25	95	82	67	27	14	11	18	9	348 (59.1%)
Total	28	108	132	118	68	36	31	42	26	589
	(4.8%)	(18.3%)	(22.4%)	(20.0%)	(11.5%)	(6.1%)	(5.3%)	(7.1%)	(4.4%)	(100%)

TABLE 5

Number of Students by Sex and Parental Education

| Sex | Level of Parental Education [a] | | | | | | | | Total |
	No Formal Schooling	Some Primary Education	Graduate Primary School	Some Secondary Education	Graduate Secondary School	Some University Education	Graduate University	Post-University Education	
Male	49	82	59	22	8	12	4	1	237 (40.7%)
Female	33	119	90	58	27	2	10	6	345 (59.3%)
Total	82	201	149	80	35	14	14	7	582
	(14.1%)	(34.5%)	(25.6%)	(13.7%)	(6.0%)	(2.4%)	(2.4%)	(1.2%)	(100%)

[a]Father's education level was used to measure this variable.

26

permitted women from relatively high family status groups to express through teaching a concern for social welfare (Havighurst and Gouveia, 1969). It appears that men of high status or high educational background, in this sample and in Havighurst and Gouveia's study, are more attracted to professions of higher prestige and income. Males, however, still outnumber females about two to one in the secondary school teaching force of Venezuela. This trend is apparently changing, since current enrollment in the pedagogic institutes indicates a trend in favor of women over men (*Memoria y Cuenta,* 1972; *Más y Mejor,* 1970).

B. Age (Question 120)

The mean age of the total sample was approximately twenty-five years, the age median was twenty-four years.

1) *Institution.* The sample was distributed similarly across institutions with 61 percent of the total sample falling between nineteen and twenty-four years of age, and 79 percent of the total sample being twenty-six years of age or younger (table 6).[5]

2) *Year-in-school and major.* As might be expected, the mean age of students increased with year in school. It was observed, though, that older students (twenty-eight years old and above) were found in equal proportion in all four classes. There did not appear to be any changing trend influencing the propensity of older (above twenty-eight) students to return for a university degree. That is, it is as likely to find as many twenty-eight-year-old students entering the first-year class as are found in the fourth-year class. The ages of students were generally similar when analyzed by major. In other words, there was an approximately equal proportion of younger and older students found in each special area of study.

3) *Parental education.* In terms of the education level of parents, students whose parents had a secondary education or higher were

[5]A variation occurred in the age distribution of the sample drawn from Central University (38 percent were 30 years of age or older). This variation resulted from drawing a major portion of the Central University sample from an evening class (the only evening class sampled in this study). It was observed that many of these individuals were teachers returning for preparation as administrators and were, therefore, somewhat older than students at other institutions sampled.

TABLE 6

Number of Students by Age and Institution

Years of Age	Institution						Total
	Andrés Bello	Central University	Pedagogic Institute Caracas	Pedagogic Institute Barquisimeto	Los Andes University	University of the Oriente	
17-18	0	1	12	14	2	0	29 (4.9%)
19-20	0	4	67	36	2	0	109 (18.3%)
21-22	4	9	65	33	16	5	132 (22.2%)
23-24	7	15	36	43	15	4	120 (20.2%)
25-26	2	6	27	17	13	3	68 (11.4%)
27-28	0	8	12	12	4	0	36 (6.1%)
29-30	2	5	9	12	4	0	32 (5.4%)
31-35	3	9	7	20	3	0	42 (7.1%)
36 and over	1	12	2	5	6	1	27 (4.5%)
Total	19 (3.2%)	69 (11.6%)	237 (39.8%)	192 (32.3%)	65 (10.9%)	13 (2.2%)	595 (100%)

virtually all below the age of twenty-six. Although this category included only sixty-eight students it may suggest that students from higher-educated families have only recently begun to select secondary education as a career. It may also reflect the rather recent development of mass higher educational opportunity in Venezuela; the children of parents educated fifteen to twenty years ago, before the period when access to education was increased, are just now of university attendance age. These students are part of a new generation in Venezuela; the true and total impact they will have on education and society has yet to be seen. Another phenomenon partly responsible for these societal changes may be the increased value that is placed on education per se as educational opportunity and experience are increased. Career aspirations that value education may be influenced by greater educational participation of the parents.

C. Civil Status (Question 121)

Approximately three-quarters of the students were single, 23 percent were married of whom 17 percent had children.[6] The pedagogic institutes accounted for a higher percentage of single students while Central University was represented by a considerably higher-than-average number of married students with children (corresponding to the older population sampled). A higher proportion of single students were female while the majority of married students with children were males. It is assumed that men are more likely to return to school after beginning a family than women, since the women are charged with the child-rearing function in the home. It may also be assumed that males, upon finishing secondary school, have the alternative of pursuing other activities and later returning to complete their education, whereas females are more likely to continue their education immediately upon secondary school graduation. They are less likely to reenter school after they marry and begin having children. A higher proportion of married students with children majored in humanities, pedagogy, and counseling-evaluation-administration. Married

---

[6] Albornoz (1965) reported that in his sample of Venezuelan primary school teachers, predominantly female, 52 percent were married, while Gross et al. (1968) reported that 64 percent of the predominantly female primary teachers in Ciudad Guayana were married.

29

students had parents with considerably less formal education than single students, an observation that relates to the higher age of students with less-schooled parents mentioned above.

D. Residency (Question 122)

Approximately half the students sampled reported living with their parents and the other half with relatives, as head of their own household, alone, or with peers. Males and older students were more likely to live alone or with their spouse (own household). One observes that familial ties remain strong for university-level students.[7] Although it is not known whether this pattern is better explained by geographic proximity, financial security, or value orientations, relatively few single students (36 percent) live alone or with peers, away from their parents.

E. Urban-Rural Background (Question 123)

The sample was asked to report the size of the city or town where they had spent the major part of their lives while growing up. The question was designed to assess the sample in terms of rural-urban influences. The results showed that about 86 percent of the students lived in a city or town of more than two thousand inhabitants while growing up. Males tended to report coming from a rural background more frequently than females. Students who reported that their parents had graduated from secondary school or who were university educated were raised almost exclusively in urban areas.[8] The consequence of this is that prospective secondary school teachers are drawn from urban environments, and are likely influenced by urban attitudes and values, as well as by the aspirations of urban dwellers (which may explain the difficulty in getting secondary teachers to move to the rural setting).

---

[7]The fact that university-level students are more likely to live with parents has been reported in other research carried out in Latin America. For example, Williamson (1964), in a study of Colombian university students, found that some 60 percent of the students lived at home with parents.

[8]At the time of this sample there were no rural public secondary schools in Venezuela.

F. Political and Religious Convictions (Questions 68, 56)

Information concerning political and religious orientations was solicited from the sample in an attempt to identify the distribution of these value sentiments within this student population.

1) *Political convictions.* The sample population indicated some reservation about providing information concerning their political convictions: one-third of the total sample chose the response alternative of not indicating their political orientation; thirteen percent failed to respond to this question, more than double the average frequency of nonresponse. Of those who indicated their political position, one-third indicated they were politically "moderate." Individuals reporting that they were on the "left" and "extreme left" of the political spectrum came to 17 percent of the respondents and those who indicated that they were on the "right" or "extreme right" constituted only 4 percent of the sample.[9] Thus, of those who indicated a political preference, the trend was moderate and to the left. Students at Andrés Bello University were somewhat more conservative than the total sample whereas students at Central University were located toward the left end of the continuum. Forty percent of the students at the Pedagogic Institute of Barquisimeto marked "prefer not to answer." While the total history of political expression at each institution was not known, it was assumed that a higher percentage of "prefer not to answer" responses at the Pedagogic Institute in Barquisimeto resulted from distinct social forces in that environment. In other words, the political sensitivity of the local culture was, no doubt, partially responsible for the relatively high percentage of students who chose to mark this political question "prefer not to answer." In addition, the association of the questionnaire with North American investigators may have created a degree of suspicion in the respondents.[10]

More male students chose either the "leftist" or the "rightist" end of the continuum than females. Females were more likely to

---

[9] Albornoz (1965) found that in his sample of primary school teachers 35 percent indicated they were to the left, 25 percent to the right, and 40 percent in the center.

[10] Even though respondent anonymity was assured, the apparent concern for revealing sensitive information may imply a certain lack of confidence in the end purposes of this study.

prefer not to respond to the question. The moderate position on the political spectrum, however, was marked equally by males and females.

Younger students tended to prefer not to mark a political preference. On the other hand, as age increased there was a tendency for older students to mark a preference on one or the other extreme of the political expectrum suggesting that older students may not be as politically moderate. It may also suggest that as age increases there is a tendency to increase one's ability to express political preference without as much concern for how the information will be used.

2) *Religious convictions.* In terms of religious preference, 80 percent of the sample reported being Catholic, 3 percent Protestant, and 2 percent a religion other than the two mentioned; 15 percent claimed no religion. All students at Andrés Bello University reported being Catholic while a relatively high percentage of students at Central University and the University of the Oriente indicated they had no religion. The small percentage of Protestants in the sample was drawn almost exclusively from the two pedagogic institutes. More males than females professed no religion.

When religious preference is controlled by parental education, a trend emerges. Among students whose parents have little or no formal education, as well as among students whose parents have some university education, the preference for no religion remains relatively constant and in agreement with the overall 15 percent of the sample who claimed no religious preference. The percentage of such individuals tends to decline, however, when parents are reported to have graduated from secondary school, and tends to increase dramatically among students whose parents have graduated from university. It may be posited that as level of parental education increases through the secondary level, students tend to become more religious, whereas when parental education goes beyond the secondary level, there is a marked increase in the number of students who claim no religion.

III. Family Background (Appendix C)

A. Parental Education (Questions 126, 128)

Questions concerning the educational background of the students' parents were included in the questionnaire.[11] Seventy-five percent of the students reported that their fathers had a primary education or less and 80 percent indicated that their mothers had a primary education or less. Approximately 50 percent of both mothers and fathers had not graduated from primary school. Although the educational level of both parents is low in comparison with their university-trained children, males are currently exceeding females in terms of the level of education achieved by their respective parents. It may be posited that higher education is currently attracting more males, or that males are receiving more encouragement to attend the university. The older students report that their parents have less education than their younger schoolmates.[12]

The rather low level of education achieved by parents among this sample is consistent with two earlier studies concerned with attitudes of Venezuelan primary school teachers. Albornoz (1965), in a study of 457 teachers found 70 percent reported that their parents had completed primary school or less while Gross et

[11]An additional set of questions concerning the occupation of the father (Appendix R, 124, 125) presented several problems. First, although the respondents were asked to give the father's job title and to describe what he did while working at his job, neither question was successful in soliciting sufficient classifiable information. Although almost the entire sample responded to this set of questions, the information provided did not enable a valid and reliable category system to be developed. In other words, the majority responded with too abstract a definition of the occupation and it became impossible to differentiate between a farmer and a large landholder, for example, or a small and large businessman. The second problem began to emerge as we attempted to classify those occupations which were sufficiently definitive. Owing to the lack of available prior research utilizing socioeconomic analyses in Venezuela, this task began to rely more upon our North American biases than on a realistic appraisal of the Venezuelan class structure. It is hoped that future researchers will keep these points in mind and will find useful not only our experience but the data reported later concerning rankings of a set of occupations on a scale in accord with the prestige associated with each. Perhaps such a ranking will assist in the development of a scale suitable for future socioeconomic analyses.

[12]This age difference may relate to the lack of educational facilities available in rural Venezuela before the late 1950s and the accompanying urbanization process endemic during that and later periods.

33

al. (1968), in a study of primary teachers in Ciudad Guyana, found that 85 percent of the fathers and 92 percent of the mothers had completed primary school or less.

B. Employment of Mothers (Question 127)

An additional indicator of family background, the percentage of mothers working regularly outside the home, was included in the questionnaire. Although only 15 percent of the students reported that their mothers worked regularly outside the home, two factors make this finding important. First, students reporting working mothers tended to be young, under the age of twenty-two. Second, a somewhat higher percentage of working mothers, as opposed to nonworking mothers, had a secondary education or more.

One may posit that the more highly educated the mothers of these students, the more likely they are to be working. The phenomenon of working mothers may relate to increasing opportunities for educated women to work in urban areas. It is difficult to present verifiable explanations of the social changes that are taking place in Venezuela and other complex modernizing societies. The high preference for expanding preschool education reported in the next chapter may indicate a trend toward the increasing use of the schools for custodial care, thus providing more freedom for mothers to work. On the other hand, the popularity of child development notions that promote the early exposure of children to social and learning environments may be the force that accounts for a high valuing of preschooling. It does seem that both the desire for preschooling and the increasing employment of women in the labor market are associated, perhaps interdependently, with behaviors that are reflected in urbanization, "modernizing" values, and other social phenomena that accompany twentieth-century industrialized society.

C. Parental Place of Birth (Question 129)

In order to assess the participation of second-generation immigrants in Venezuelan higher education, and compare the attitudes of this group to nationals, a question concerning the place of birth of parents was asked. The results showed that

12 percent of the sample had one or both parents born outside Venezuela.

The highest percentage of foreign-born parents was found in Andrés Bello University leading to speculation that there exists among foreign-born Catholics an orientation toward private education under the auspices of the Church. There was also a relatively higher percentage of foreign-born parents reported by technical-vocational majors which may suggest an orientation toward the skilled-labor occupational sector. Since both cases are drawn from small segments of the total population, they should be viewed here as hypotheses for further study rather than as trends.[13]

IV. Student Employment (Appendix D, Questions 63, 64, 65)

The set of questions on student employment was designed to assess the proportion of Venezuelan education students enrolled at the university level who were employed. Forty-three percent of the sample said they were employed during the 1970-71 academic year. The two institutions enrolling part-time evening students, Andrés Bello and Central University, had a higher proportion of students who held jobs. Male students and older students were more likely to work. A higher percentage of third- and fourth-year students than first- and second-year students reported holding jobs.

1) *Hours worked per week.* Of those who reported working, approximately 50 percent were working twenty hours or less per week, 22 percent reported working less than ten hours per week, and 17 percent reported working thirty-six hours or more per week. Women tended to work fewer hours per week than males, and younger students worked fewer hours per week than did older students.

2) *Type of employment.* The majority of the students who worked indicated that they were involved in either primary or

---

[13]Future investigations might attempt an assessment of the background of immigrants and their children's motivations for pursuing particular careers. In addition, one might study such immigrants in terms of their value orientations as "deviants" in the modernization process promoting, perhaps, career socialization patterns distinct from those of nationals (Lipset, 1967; Bonilla, 1970).

secondary school teaching, the two job categories accounting for 82 percent of the working students. Women tended to report working at the primary level whereas men were more often found working at the secondary level. The tendency was for younger students to be employed in primary schools and older students to be employed in secondary schools. Some differentiation by major was also found with humanities students employed more frequently in primary schools and natural science students more frequently in secondary schools. In terms of the level of education completed by parents, there was a trend among children of less-educated parents to teach in primary schools, whereas children of more-educated parents were more likely to be teaching in secondary schools.

V. Secondary School Background (Appendix E)

1) *Year of graduation from secondary school (Question 37).* About 57 percent of the sample had graduated from secondary school between 1966 and 1971. The students who had graduated before this time were more likely to be found in Central University and the University of the Andes. Women tended to constitute the more recent secondary school graduating classes while men tended to constitute a majority of those graduating ten or more years before.

2) *Geographic location of the secondary school (Question 38).* The location of the secondary school from which students graduated was generally found to relate to attendance at a university in the same immediate geographical area. The only variant to this generalization appeared in the case of students attending Central University where about 51 percent were from schools located in the Caracas area, and 21 percent were from secondary schools located in the Oriente region. Of the thirty-seven students who reported having parents with postsecondary education, twenty-six reported attending secondary schools in the Caracas area.

3) *Sponsoring agency of the secondary school (Question 40).* Of the total sample, 81 percent of the students indicated that they had attended federal or state public secondary schools while

14 percent indicated that they had attended private Catholic schools. Of the six universities included in the sample only Andrés Bello differed considerably from the others in terms of the percentage of students who had attended private Catholic secondary schools. Between 12 percent and 15 percent of the sample in the other institutions reported having attended such schools while in Andrés Bello University about 62 percent of the sample indicated that they had attended private Catholic secondary institutions. The majority, or 69 percent, of those who attended private Catholic secondary schools were women. No relationship was noted between level of education achieved by parents and attendance at a private or public secondary school.

4) *Type of secondary school (Question 41)*. About 75 percent of the total sample graduated from a secondary school of the academic type while 19 percent graduated from a normal school. A higher percentage of normal school graduates were enrolled in the two pedagogic institutes whereas the academic school graduates were distributed evenly across all institutions. Normal school graduates tended to be older than academic graduates with 50 percent of the former and 17 percent of the latter being twenty-eight years of age or older, suggesting that normal school graduates are more likely to embark on their careers as elementary teachers for a period of time before returning to the university for an advanced degree. It also suggests that a number of elementary school teachers are switching to secondary school teaching after several years of experience on the job.

Commercial school and technical-vocational school graduates accounted for 3 percent and 2 percent of the sample, respectively. These students tended to major in the same subject matter at the university level that had attracted them at the secondary level. Normal school graduates, on the other hand, tended to major at the university in pedagogy, counseling-evaluation-administration, or humanities. Among academic secondary school graduates about 42 percent of the cohort was enrolled in the physical and natural sciences.

More than 75 percent of the students whose parents had more than a secondary education attended academic secondary institutions. The data indicated that there was a lower percentage of parents who had less than a primary school education among

37

commercial school graduates than among any other secondary school graduates.

5) *Secondary school major (Question 42)*. At the secondary level about 46 percent of the sample majored in one of the sciences (mathematics, biology, and physics) while 28 percent majored in humanities and 19 percent were normal school majors. Science majors tended to enroll at one of the pedagogic institutes or at the University of Oriente whereas humanities majors tend to enroll at either Andrés Bello or Central University.

The data suggest that a student's major at the secondary level is related to his university major. For example, science majors in the secondary school are likely to enroll in the sciences at the university, while humanities majors are equally distributed across pedagogy, counseling-evaluation-administration, humanities, and languages. Normal school graduates are more likely found in the same majors as humanities students with the exception of languages. Secondary school technical-vocational and commercial majors are also prone to major in the same specializations at the university. There was no relationship noted among level of education completed by parents and secondary school major; instead, the distribution was found to be relatively equal across all majors.

6) *Size of secondary school graduating class (Question 43)*. A question regarding secondary school background inquired into the size of an individual's secondary school graduating class. The results indicated that 40 percent graduated in a class of between 26 and 50 students, 25 percent graduated in a class of 51 to 100 students, 25 percent in a class of 100 students or more, and 11 percent in a class of fewer than 25 students.

Chapter Three
Professional Expectations
and Orientations

The cost of preparing a secondary school teacher, counselor, or administrator is considerable both to the nation and to the individual. Wastage often occurs in the training of individuals in both professional and technical fields when those trained either voluntarily or involuntarily choose alternative careers where their training is not of practical use. Experienced teachers frequently choose to leave teaching after being in the profession for a relatively short period of time, thereby increasing the cost to the nation. In addition, teacher training institutions and departments of education within universities often attribute to students certain professional and personal attitudes toward the profession only to learn that those attitudes do not match institutional expectations among graduates in the field.

For these reasons, a series of questions was asked in order to assess the goals, plans, and orientations of education students being prepared as professional educators at the secondary level. The questions were designed to elicit where the individual intended to work by region and type of school, the position sought inside or outside a school, whether additional income through a second job would be necessary, and the anticipated involvement in the administration of the school where the individual planned to work. Included were questions concerning teacher union membership and the teaching of religion in school.

A. Employment Aspirations and Expectations (Appendix F)

1) *Intentions to work in secondary schools (Question 45).* In response to the question, "Do you plan on working in the secondary schools when you graduate from this university?" 94 percent of the sample answered in the affirmative. A somewhat higher percentage of those students enrolled in the two pedagogic institutes and the University of the Andes indicated they were planning to work in a secondary school, whereas only 80 percent

responded in the affirmative among students at Andrés Bello, Central and Oriente Universities. Males outnumbered females among those who indicated that they were not inclined to work in secondary schools upon graduation. Also noted in the results was a tendency for pedagogy and counseling-evaluation-administration majors to be less inclined to work in a secondary school. Although students who were not inclined to work in secondary schools amounted to only 15 percent of each of the majors mentioned above, this percentage deviates from the total sample by major. Almost 30 percent of the students whose parents had some university education or higher indicated they did not intend working in secondary schools upon graduation.

One may hypothesize that males majoring in pedagogy and counseling-evaluation-administration are likely to take positions in their fields of preparation in other than secondary institutions or that they intend pursuing their studies in an allied field at a university. Since a relatively high percentage of those who do not intend working in a secondary school have parents with higher education backgrounds it may be assumed that they are inclined to pursue further formal education at the university level.

2) *Position sought inside or outside the secondary school (Questions 47, 46).* The highest percentage of those students who reported that they did not intend working in secondary schools indicated a desire to pursue further studies (31 percent). A lower percentage indicated that they would teach at another level (21 percent), go into administration (17 percent), or conduct research (10 percent). Thus, the majority of the 6 percent of the sample who indicated they would not work in a secondary institution will apparently pursue careers entirely related to the wider concerns of education as a profession.

Of the individuals who indicated that they would work in secondary schools, approximately three-quarters reported that they intended to become either a full- or part-time teacher while 12 percent intended to become administrators, 5 percent counselors, and 3 percent test and measurement specialists. The intentions of students varied by institution: about 19 percent of the students at Andrés Bello and Central University, along with 12 percent at each of the pedagogic institutes, were planning to pursue careers as administrators. The last statistic is especially striking for students enrolled in the pedagogic institutes since a special curriculum designed to prepare secondary school administrators is not offered at these schools.

Twenty-five percent of the students at the University of the Andes and 10 percent of the students at Central University were planning to become counselors whereas 21 percent of the students at the University of the Andes and 7 percent of those at Andrés Bello were planning to become specialists in tests and measurement.

The data suggest that as students become older and as they move through their university careers there is a marked decrease in the desire to become teachers; for older students there is a marked increase in the desire to pursue careers as administrators and counselors. Thus, it may be posited that education students tend to move away from teaching as a career and into other educational specialties as they increase in age. Owing to the number of older students in the sample returning to the universities as part-time students, however, it may be hypothesized that of those individuals who have had experience as teachers, an increasing percentage tend to pursue careers leading to work as counselors and administrators.

In terms of work preferences by major, students preferring positions as administrators tended to be rather equally distributed among all majors, while those bent on pursuing careers in counseling and tests and measurements were usually enrolled in those majors.

3) *Long-term commitment to teaching (Questions 60, 61).* In an attempt to measure the intensity of the sample's commitment to teaching as a profession, the students were asked whether or not they would be teaching five years hence, and if not, what they would be doing. The results indicated that 85 percent of the sample thought they would still be teaching.[1] Comparing this

[1]Gross et al. (1968) asked their sample of primary school teachers in Ciudad Guayana two similar questions. In response to what the teachers (average of seven years' teaching experience for the sample) would hope to do five years hence, 20 percent indicated they would leave the field of education, 33 percent would remain in teaching, and 39 percent would hope to be a school principal. When asked the same question for a ten-year period, 25 percent indicated they would leave the field of education. Albornoz (1965) found that 23 percent of the primary school teachers he sampled desired to change occupations at the time of the administration of the questionnaire (41 percent had taught less than five years and 46 percent had taught between six and fifteen years).

response with that of a prior question concerning whether the students intended to become teachers, it is noted that approximately fifty individuals who were planning to pursue careers as teachers did not plan to be teaching five years hence. Students at the Pedagogic Institute in Caracas, along with students from the total sample enrolled in the first and second years of their university careers, were more likely to think that they would remain in teaching for a minimum of five years. In addition, those students whose parents had university training or higher indicated that they would be less likely to be teaching in five years.

The majority of the ninety-one students, or 15 percent of the sample, who indicated that they would not be teaching in five years were planning to pursue further studies at a university. Lower percentages planned either to teach at a level other than secondary or to pursue research.

The results suggest that the commitment to teaching is high, very likely higher than the actuality will prove to be five years from now. Thus, although the number of teachers who actually remain in teaching for a five-year period in Venezuela, as elsewhere, is likely to be small, the intentions of students studying to become teachers cannot be used as a reason to explain the turnover.

4) *Preference for subject to be taught in secondary schools (Question 69).* Of those students who planned to teach after graduation, the respondents were queried as to which subject they would prefer teaching. The question was designed to assess the number of students planning to teach the subject for which they were being prepared. The results indicated that students majoring in a field of study which was teachable as a subject in secondary schools generally intended to teach that subject, whereas, the majority of those students majoring in pedagogy or counseling-administration-evaluation intended to teach humanities. Thus, of those not majoring in subject matter areas normally taught at the secondary level, there is a strong tendency to prefer humanities, a subject presumably more likely to accommodate varied professional backgrounds.

5) *Preference for type of secondary school (Questions 66, 67).* In addition to our inquiry into the teaching plans of those who

42

intended to teach at the secondary level, information was solicited regarding the type of institution preferred. The question asked the sample to check academic, commercial, agriculture, vocational/technical, normal, or "other" as the preferred institution. The data suggested that over 75 percent of the sample planned to teach at academic secondary schools with the remaining students choosing a technical-vocational, normal, or commercial school. Of those who did not intend working at an academic school, 20 percent of the students at Central University and a somewhat lower percentage at Los Andes University preferred a technical-vocational school. About 40 percent of the students at Andrés Bello University intended to work at normal schools. Students choosing a normal school were generally older than the others and were likely to be majors in either pedagogy or humanities.

Students majoring in subjects commonly taught in the secondary school preferred to teach at the academic secondary schools and those majoring in technical/vocational and commercial subjects preferred the technical/vocational and commercial secondary schools, respectively. Of those students preferring to teach at technical/vocational secondary schools, however, 25 percent represented pedagogy majors, 23 percent counseling-administration-evaluation majors, 19 percent physical science majors, and only 12 percent technical/vocational majors. Students with parents who had less than a secondary school education tended to prefer normal schools or technical/vocational schools.

About 94 percent of the sample preferred to teach in public schools and only 3 percent in private schools. Perhaps work conditions, job security, and other benefits such as retirement pay in the public system contribute to this bias. The small, private school preference emanated from females and primarily from Andrés Bello University. Pedagogy, counseling-administration-evaluation, and natural science majors constituted nearly all of those students who preferred private schools.

6) *Additional employment for teachers (Questions 48, 49).* As has long been a tradition in Latin America, teachers at the secondary and higher education levels often have more than one job in order not only to secure a sufficient wage but also to meet the demand for individuals with their background and professional preparation. Education observers in Latin America, however, have

noted a growing trend among teachers at both levels to be engaged full-time at only one institution.[2] In an attempt to assess this trend, students were asked whether or not they felt they would have to earn additional income after becoming a teacher, and if so, what type of work they thought they would do for that additional income.

The responses indicated that about 31 percent of the sample thought they would have to earn income in addition to their jobs as teachers. Men tended to respond with an intent to moonlight more than women. Technical/vocational, commercial, and counseling-administration-evaluation majors were more likely to seek additional income, whereas, humanities majors were less likely to seek such income.

Of those who intended to moonlight, some 40 percent thought they would be teachers while 32 percent thought they would be engaged in business or commerce. There was no apparent pattern by major among students who preferred to teach whereas counseling-evaluation-administration and commercial majors tended toward business or commercial occupations and humanities majors toward positions involving writing or journalism.

7) *Preference for teaching by geographic locale (Questions 70, 71).* Two questions were designed to assess student preferences for the geographical location where they would prefer to and where they expected to teach. Approximately one-third of the sample preferred to teach in Caracas, 19 percent in Barquisimeto, 2 percent in the San Cristobal area, 30 percent in another major city, and 12 percent in a small city or town.

Students who preferred Caracas were drawn primarily from the two pedagogic institutes while those who preferred another large city were from the two institutes plus the University of the Andes. Of students enrolled in institutions located in Caracas, the majority preferred to teach in Caracas whereas those enrolled in the Pedagogic Institute at Barquisimeto preferred Barquisimeto. The majority of students enrolled in Los Andes and Oriente Universities indicated a preference for teaching at a large city other than Caracas, Barquisimeto, or San Cristóbal. The students

---

[2]The study of primary teachers in Ciudad Guayana by Gross et al. (1968) found that only 5 percent of the predominantly female sample had outside jobs.

44

preferring a small city or town were enrolled in the Pedagogic Institute at Caracas or at Central University. At the same time, of those students enrolled at Central University and the Pedagogic Institute at Caracas, 30 percent and 16 percent, respectively, would prefer to work in a small city or town.

Viewing the same data in a somewhat different way, students enrolled in the three Caracas institutions preferred working in the Capital District while 35 percent of the enrollees of the Pedagogic Institute at Barquisimeto accounted for 85 percent of those preferring to work in the Central Western region. Forty-five percent of those choosing to work in the Andes region were enrolled at the University of the Andes while 17 percent preferring to work in the Northeast region were enrolled at either the University of Oriente or the Pedagogic Institute of Caracas. Overall, 37 percent of the sample preferred to teach in the Capital, 20 percent in the Central Western, 14 percent in the Andes, 9 percent in the Central, 8 percent in the Northeast, 5 percent in Zulia, and 2 percent in Guayana.

In addition to an apparent relationship among the location of the enrollee's university, his family residence, and where he seeks employment, when the sample was asked where they expected to teach rather than preferred to teach, 81 percent indicated that their expectation was the same as their preference. Thus, either students tend to feel they can find positions in the locale of their choice or they prefer and expect to teach at a locale where they know positions will be available.

B. Teachers' Unions (Appendix G)

Relatively little is known about whether or not teachers in Latin America find teachers' unions necessary and if they do find them necessary what service they provide to assist and support teachers.

1) *Intention to join a teachers' union (Question 72).* Students were asked whether or not they would join the teachers' union after they got a job teaching. Seventy-five percent of the respondents indicated they would, whereas, 2 percent responded "no" and 23 percent answered that they had not considered the question sufficiently to respond. A considerably higher percentage

of men answered in the affirmative. Younger students as well as students enrolled in the first two years of their university careers were more likely to respond that they were unsure whether they would join the union.[3]

2) *The need for teachers' unions (Questions 58, 59).* Students were asked whether they thought teachers' unions were necessary. About 98 percent answered in the affirmative. The small percentage of the sample responding "no" was from the two pedagogic institutes and tended to be in the first two years of school and majoring in either humanities or the physical sciences.

With respect to why the students thought unions were necessary, the sample was asked to check one of the following: to improve conditions of work for teachers, to improve schools for children, to support teaching as a profession, or to specify another reason. The majority (52 percent) indicated that unions were essential in order to improve schools for children, 24 percent indicated that they were necessary in order to support teaching as a profession, and 23 percent thought that unions were necessary to improve work conditions for professors. Women predominated among students who thought that unions were important in order to improve work conditions, whereas men predominated among those who thought that unions were important in order to defend teaching as a profession.

C. Teacher-Administrator Relationships (Appendix H)

1) *Involvement in school administration (Question 50).* In order to assess student expectations regarding teacher involvement in the administration of a secondary school, the students in the sample were asked what they thought their involvement would be with the administration of the school where they would teach. They were given the following response choices: expect to participate in policy and planning decisions; expect to be consulted only regarding matters concerning me; expect to be permitted to offer my opinion; or do not expect to actively participate in administrative affairs. Sixty-eight percent indicated that they thought

---

[3] Albornoz (1965) found that 71 percent of the primary teachers sampled belonged to the primary school teachers' union in Venezuela (Federación Venezolana de Maestros).

they should be permitted to express their opinion, 18 percent hoped they would be able to participate in decisions on policy and planning, while 12 percent indicated that they would expect to be consulted only in relation to matters that concerned them. Students at Andrés Bello and Central Universities exceeded by far the mean percentage response in terms of expecting to be able to participate in decisions on policy and planning.

2) *Involvement with the Ministry of Education (Question 51).* In order to provide the sample with an opportunity to more realistically appraise their intentions relative to administrative participation, the students were asked the following question: "Suppose a ruling were being considered by the Ministry of Education which you felt would be harmful to education in Venezuela. If you expressed your opinion on the ruling to an official of the Ministry, how do you think he would react? " Students were asked to mark one of the following: he would give your point of view serious consideration; he would pay some attention to your point of view; he would pay only little attention to your point of view; or, he would ignore what you had to say.

About 36 percent replied that the official would pay some attention to his opinion; 24 percent replied that the official would pay little attention to his opinion; and 19 percent replied that the official would totally ignore what he said. Students from Andrés Bello University, no doubt because one of their professors was Director of Secondary and Higher Education for the Ministry of Education, exceeded the mean sample percentage of those who believed the official would pay some attention to their opinions. Of those responding that the official would totally ignore what they said, men predominated, while of those responding that the official would pay some attention to their opinions, women predominated. A decreasing preference until age thirty-two was noted for the category that some attention would be paid to his opinion. At age thirty-two, the category tended to increase in preference. Pedagogy and humanities majors tended to prefer "some attention would be paid;" counseling-evaluation-administration majors tended to favor "serious regard would be paid;" and physical science majors tended to prefer "opinion would be ignored."

47

3) *Influencing the Ministry (Question 52).* To test the intensity of attitudes regarding expressing one's opinion to a ministerial official, the following question was asked: "If such a case arose, how likely is it that you would actually try to influence the ministry? " About 39 percent replied somewhat likely; 15 percent, very likely; 6 percent, somewhat unlikely; 7 percent, very unlikely; and 32 percent did not know. Thus, 54 percent of the total group felt that they would attempt to influence an official from the Ministry.

When compared with the norm established by all institutions, there was a tendency for students from Andrés Bello University to indicate that it would be somewhat unlikely or very unlikely that they would try to influence an official from the Ministry. Men predominated among students who thought it was somewhat unlikely that they would try to influence an official of the Ministry. Students in their later years in school, when compared with those in their first year, tended to feel that it would be very unlikely that they would attempt to influence the official. Among the respective majors, those in pedagogy thought it was very unlikely while those in natural science thought that it was somewhat likely that they would attempt to influence a ministerial official.

4) *Value conflict in response to a request for teaching certain material (Question 57).* In an attempt to approach somewhat circuitously the issue of administrative involvement, reference is made here to an attitudinal item that relates to what a person would do if asked to teach material that contradicted some of his own values and beliefs. The responses included: refuse to teach it or just omit it; ask to have someone else teach it; teach it, but give your own viewpoint; try to teach it objectively, giving both sides; teach it as requested, keeping your own viewpoint entirely out of it. The highest percentage of the sample (41 percent) indicated that they would teach the material but would also present their own point of view. The remaining students indicated that they would either try to teach the material objectively, presenting alternative points of view (26 percent) or would teach the material as requested, excluding their points of view (22 percent). Less than 10 percent of the sample would either omit the material or ask someone else to teach it.

Among the responses by institution, students at Andrés Bello tended to exceed the other institutional norms in the categories "omit the material" and "present both sides," while students at Central University exceeded the norms for other institutions in the category, "present my own point of view." Of those who indicated "refuse to teach it or just omit it," males predominated over females.

When viewing the sample's response by age and year in school, there was a tendency for younger students to place more importance on presenting "my own point of view," whereas older students and those enrolled in their later years of school tended to prefer "giving both sides."

D. Religion and Teaching (Appendix I)

An important concern of all societies in the education of children relates to the teaching of moral and ethical values. In societies that draw heavily on institutionalized religion, such as Catholicism in Venezuela, it often implies that teachers should reflect the orientations of the dominant religion and mirror that influence through their behavior in and out of the classroom.

1) *Religious convictions (Questions 56, 55).* To assess the religious orientations of the sample, four questions were posed regarding religious membership, religious convictions, the importance of such convictions for teachers, and whether or not religion should be taught in school. The first question, concerning religious membership, was reported in the preceding chapter. Briefly, 80 percent were Catholic, 3 percent Protestant, 2 percent another religion, and 15 percent claimed no religion.

On religious convictions, the sample was asked to check the response that best reflected their particular orientation. The responses included: I do not have any religious faith (14 percent); I consider myself religious, but do not take part in formal religious services (42 percent); I occasionally attend religious services (23 percent); I participate regularly in religious services (16 percent); I am profoundly religious and always try to participate in religious activities (6 percent). Thus, the results suggest that about 56 percent either have no religious faith or are religious but do not take part in formal religious services.

More students at Andrés Bello University than at the others participated in religious activities. Males were more likely to report not having any religious beliefs whereas females tended to predominate among those who reported being profoundly religious. Third-year students and students enrolled as physical science majors exceeded the norm for those who claimed no religious beliefs.

A trend emerged among the religious convictions reported and the level of education achieved by parents. As parental education increased through the secondary level, the percentage of students who professed no religious beliefs and those who claimed religious beliefs but did not participate in religious services decreased, whereas the percentage of those who indicated that they participated on a regular basis tended to increase. A similar observation was made in the preceding chapter in that students who claimed no religion declined as parental education increased through the secondary level.

2) *Importance of religious beliefs for teachers (Question 54).* To draw upon religious convictions and beliefs in terms of their importance for education, students were asked the following question: "In your opinion, what importance does religious faith and belief have for the good teacher? " The following responses were presented and students were asked to check the most appropriate: it is essential (12 percent); it helps (38 percent); it is not important (33 percent); it does not help (9 percent); or, it hinders (9 percent). Thus, about half indicated that religious faith and belief are of some importance for the good teacher and half such faith and belief are not important for the good teacher. Of students who felt that religious faith and belief were not important, males outnumbered females. About 90 percent of the students at Andrés Bello University indicated that religious beliefs and faith were either essential or helpful, whereas about 39 percent of the students at Central University believed that such orientations were either essential or helpful.

3) *Religious instruction in the schools (Question 19).* The last inquiry concerning religion read as follows: "Religion should be taught in school." The sample was asked to mark strongly agree, agree, disagree, or strongly disagree. The responses showed that

about 60 percent of the population disagreed with the statement. The results of a multivariate analysis indicated a significant difference (>0.0001) between males and females in response to this statement. Females registered more agreement with the statement than males. For example, of those who were in complete agreement with the statement, 28 percent were males and 72 percent were females, while of those who were in complete disagreement with the statement 60 percent were males and 40 percent were females.[4]

As was true with previous questions concerning religion, a trend was present when the responses were viewed by the level of education achieved by parents. Viewing the trend in terms of agreement with the statement, about 29 percent of the students whose parents had no formal education were in agreement whereas 65 percent of those students whose parents graduated from secondary school were agreed that religion should be taught in school.

[4] Albornoz (1960) found that 429 of the 457 primary school teachers in his sample claimed to be Catholics and that 65 percent thought religion should be taught at all levels of the primary school. Gross et al. (1968) found that 85 percent of the primary teachers thought that religious instruction (and sex education) should definitely or probably be the responsibility of the school.

Chapter Four
Venezuelan Educational Needs and National Development Priorities

I. Venezuelan Educational Needs (Appendix J)

Six items were included in the questionnaire which would provide a general assessment of the opinions of the students concerning the educational needs of their country, and illuminate perceived deficiencies in the present system. These questions attempt an evaluation of education couched in terms of existent problems. It is hoped that the responses can be juxtaposed against philosophical and attitudinal statements in order to analyze the apparent consistency and broader contextual meaning of such predispositions. Because this investigation is concerned primarily with individual attitudes and not with an evaluation of the educational system, these data were gathered to provide a basis for the analysis of both individual philosophies of education and the role of education in Venezuela.

A secondary purpose for gathering this normative data, however, is to enable one to make at least a preliminary comment concerning the perceived effectiveness of the present educational system. While it was not the purpose of this study to broach policy questions, the results of the survey do have definite and important implications for Venezuelan education. There is an intensive concern in Venezuela, as in other nations of the world, for planning educational futures. The selection of criteria and priorities for educational plans must be based upon both public and professional desire and demand as well as upon reasoned exigencies.

The opinions of the segment of the population that has been sampled in this research are particularly important to consider in policy formulation. These individuals have immediate experience as students and have participated in the total system of schooling, primary school through university. They are also those who are committed to the process and system of education, preparing to become professional educators. As future teachers, administrators,

52

and specialists they will be in a position to influence the instructional process if not the educational system itself. While it is clear that those who will depend upon the institution for their own welfare must reflect certain protective biases, the fact that the choice of education as a career was an individual one reflects the confidence that they have in the existing structure (regardless of where such attitudes were "learned"). These students are not yet locked in to the system and it can be that their opinions are those of friendly observers — sympathetic, yet still from outside the system. It is the critical opinion of individuals who are dedicated to the education profession which would seem to be most valuable to Venezuelan planning officials since they are the individuals who will be asked to implement policy at the school and classroom levels. It should further be remembered that while still experiencing formal education as "receivers," these students are in an advantageous position to judge the relevance and efficiency of school to the goals of the learner.

Two open-ended free response questions were asked the sample in order to elicit attitudes that were not influenced by predispositions of the authors. For reporting purposes the responses were grouped into general categories. A more precise statement concerning the divergence of opinion is derived from two companion questions which are also reported below.

A. The Critical Needs of Venezuelan Education (Question 8)

A free-response question asked students to report what they felt were "the three most critical needs of education in Venezuela today." The statements[1] of these students were divided into nine categories which are explained in an illustrative way below by quoting translated protocols representative of each category. Each category is identified with a descriptive statement suggesting the priority area.

---

[1] There were a total of forty-four nonrespondents to the question; eighty-seven of those who did answer provided only one or two "needs." The data indicate that rather than delimiting precise problem areas, the respondents seemingly replied from a more general frame of reference; thus, they had some difficulty in specifying as many as three responses.

1. Insufficient or ill-prepared professors and staff (27 percent); for example, mejor preparación profesional"; "se necesita mayor número de profesores"; "mayor preocupación por parte de los profesores."
2. Insufficient or inadequate schools or classes (22 percent); for example: "necesidad de otros campos de estudio"; "limitación de cupos"; "crear nuevos centros de educación superior."
3. Need for restructuring the educational system or programs (20 percent); for example: "los textos o materiales propios para la formación de los estudiantes"; "una mejor organización de los organismos educacionales"; "reforma completa – no a medias."
4. Irrelevance of education or educational technology – curriculum, values of school, etc. (10 percent); for example: "la falta de coherencia en el sistema educativo"; "cambio total de los programas de educación por considerarlos mal acoplados con la realidad actual"; "el contenido de los programas en determinadas asignaturas."
5. Problems with size or allocation of budget (6 percent); for example: "poco presupuesto o mal empleado"; "aumento del presupuesto para la educación"; "falta de recursos económicos."
6. Inattention to individual student needs or to student counseling (5 percent); for example: "falta de libertad de expresión"; "orientación de la juventud"; "la poca responsabilidad por parte de los llamados del poder joven."
7. Political inefficacies: political bias in organization and leadership of education, the need for university autonomy (5 percent); for example: "menos política en las universidades"; "acaparamiento político de los cargos educativos"; "que los políticos no intervengan en asuntos educacionales."
8. Need to improve quality of education or standards for selection of students (2 percent); for example: "dar menos materias pero de mayor cualidad"; "necesidad de mejorar el sistema educativo"; "mejoramiento del sistema de enseñanza."
9. Other unrelated responses (3 percent).

The percentage figures in parentheses represent the proportion of respondents replying in that general category in terms of an individual's *first* "most critical need." When the cumulative responses in each category were tallied for all three reported "needs," the comparative frequencies, with the exception of political inefficacy remained the same. That is, the rank order and frequency distributions of these categories remain the same (except for the one case) whether one reports the single most critical need or a mean ranking of all three of the critical needs. Ranking these results by frequency of response provided a means of comparison and minimized the effect of classifying and quantifying the responses. Comparing average rankings over three

54

choices also provided a gross measure of reliability indicating that the responses were reasonably consistent.

The category of political inefficacy in the averaged ranking of the three needs moved from seventh most reported (5 percent of first-choice responses) to fifth most reported (7 percent of averaged-choice responses), indicating that there was widespread opinion identifying it as a problem area but a secondary "need."

Categories 1 and 2, insufficient or inadequate schools and staff, were mentioned by nearly half of all respondents as the most critical need of education. Their content seems to express the need for providing more, if not better, education. It is quite possible that category 5, budget allocation, also reflects a concern for expanding education. These results, when contrasted with category 8, quality improvement and selection standards (interpreted here as reflecting attitudes of exclusivity toward schooling), clearly indicate that the former respondents favored mass education and increased educational opportunity. Given the demographic portraits of the students reported in Chapter Two, schooling has very likely served as a channel for upward mobility for this group and, thus, one may expect favorable orientations toward schools as legitimizers of social status and toward increasing opportunity and access to the schooling experience.

Categories 3 and 4 speak to the need for reforming the content or the technology of education and represented the concerns of approximately one-third of the respondents. While this statement may seem to be in conflict with the stated desire to expand (and, it is implied, maintain) the existing system, such a conclusion cannot be reached from these data. It does seem apparent, however, that there is considerable feeling on the part of the sample that organizational and curricular reforms in the educational system are needed.

B. Secondary School Reform (Question 9)

A second free-response question was asked in order to provide a more definitive answer to the general question of specifying educational needs. In it students were asked "if only one thing could be changed in relation to secondary schooling, what do you think it should be? " The qualification to *secondary* level education was made in order to specify more precise problem focuses and thereby presumably elicit a more specific response.

The issue of quantifying these data is again raised. A ranking of general response categories independent of those specified in the preceding question permitted comparisons to be made without using the same categories for the two questions. It was the decision of the authors that preserving the integrity of each question by aggregating the data separately, and then risking a larger interpretative error in comparing these results, was more descriptively productive.[2] While it is obvious that the opinions of these students are formed through experience with the same general environment, the interpretation of the meaning of these responses must be left partially to the reader.

The following categories, concerning a desire to change one thing related to secondary schools, were derived from a sampling of responses.[3] Typical protocols assist in defining the content of each category.

1. A general restructuring of the educational system (29 percent); for example: "quisiera que fuera una reforma total"; "la educación en general"; "todo."
2. Improvements in curriculum or programs (15 percent); for example: "el sistema de estudio donde todo está basado teóricamente; se debe fomentar más la práctica"; "los objetivos que ésta persigue que no estén de acuerdo con el desarrollo nacional"; "el pénsum de estudio."
3. Student participation in schools; student-teacher relationships; teaching methods (14 percent); for example: "que además de cultura general al bachiller se le vaya ayudando a escoger la carrera que más sea apto para estudiar"; "el método de enseñanza que se usa actualmente"; "las relaciones alumno-profesor."
4. Examinations and methods of evaluation (10 percent); for example: "los métodos de evaluación"; "el método de evaluación que es muy

[2] The alternative would be to construct comparable reporting categories which represent a homogeneous theoretical content. This procedure, however, would have further forced the data into arbitrary abstract constructs and away from their real content. In this research, the alternative response categories used to quantify the results were derived from an assessment of the responses themselves. The authors performed all data coding themselves so that assignment of a protocol to a response category reflects only their (hopefully cautioned) bias.

[3] There were 118 nonrespondents to this question which may again indicate that individuals were more inclined to generalize their reply to this question than to select from among a variety of alternative possible responses.

caduco y anti-humano ya que se somete al estudiante a un ambiente muy tenso"; "los exámenes finales."

5. Qualification standards for professors (9 percent); for example: "que hubiesen mejores y capacitados profesores para dirigir la educación"; "personal bien capacitado para el ejercicio de la docencia"; "que el profesional sintiera de todo corazón su labor docente."

6. Political influences (4 percent); for example: "menos ingerencia de la política en la educación"; "la política"; "cambiar la relación entre la educación y los partidos políticos."

7. Educational standards and student selection (2 percent); for example: "que haya coherencia en los estudios, es decir, que el alumno al salir de la educación secundaria pueda realizar una labor"; "desarrollar más el nivel de capacitación del individuo"; "creación de una educación que nos lleve a una culturización más profunda."

8. Other (7 percent).

It is notable that the foremost needs mentioned in the preceding question were for more educational schools and staff. There was no direct expression of this sentiment reflected in this question. While the form of the question may have solicited responses criticizing the existing system, the question itself does not preclude an individual from totally supporting additions to the existing system. It is possible that students presumed that providing more educational facilities or access to those facilities, that is, expanding the system, could only be performed outside the system; consequently they do not conceive of this need as a problem requiring change. Such an attitude reflects a rather narrow conceptualization of how schools may endogenously reconcile educational needs. On the other hand, the sample may not have felt that expansion of the secondary school system was appropriate since this question was directed specifically at the secondary level. Support for the latter interpretation is reported later in this chapter under "types of schools" where the sample appeared to concentrate their expansion orientation toward preprimary and university technical institutes.

The predominant response to this question reflected a concern for restructuring the system (29 percent) and reformulating the content of education (15 percent). These abstract and generalized responses did not serve to clarify the preceding question concerning educational needs; they did, however, substantiate a rather widespread concern for revitalizing, if not reforming, the existing educational structure. Some of the particular areas of concern were revealed by further responses to this question: student participation in educational decision making, student-teacher relationships, teaching methods, methods of evaluation and screening, qualification standards for professors, leadership, and so on.

In summary, it is important to note that these students are committed to the basic educational system and advocate its expansion and improvement. More specific indicators of the direction for such change can be gathered from the following questions.

In order to provide data that could be subjected to comparative analysis with some confidence, two forced-choice questions were asked.

C. Educational Quality (Question 53)

A variety of problematic constraints known to limit the quality of education in other areas of the world were selected and presented as response possibilities to the question: "Which three of the following factors are most influential in limiting the quality of education in Venezuela?" Students were not asked to order the importance of their responses, consequently the data are reported in order of preference by cumulative frequency. That is, the total number of individuals who considered a given factor to be one of the three most limiting factors are tallied and reported as an aggregate figure (table 7). While qualitative interfactor comparisons cannot be made with this procedure, quantitative comparisons are possible.

An apparent reordering of priorities is reflected by these data which place the area of political influence as a much more potent issue of concern than in the preceding questions. While limited financial resources and too few facilities are considered to constrain the *quality* of education, clearly of greater importance to these students is the interference of partisan politics and inadequate student-teacher contact. It might have been expected that these prospective teachers would have been more concerned with salary levels of teachers than they were, or with the role of teachers in educational decision making. It should be noted that the apparent reordering of problem areas emanating from this

TABLE 7

Factors That Limit the Quality of Education in Venezuela

Cumulative Frequency of Response[a]	Limiting Factor
402	Interference of partisan politics in educational affairs
355	Large school classes and little contact between teachers and pupils
278	Limited economic expenditures in support of education
246	Lack of teaching materials and facilities for efficient teaching
172	Disinterest by teachers in keeping up-to-date in their teaching fields
135	Lack of interest on the part of students
120	Inadequate representation of teachers in educational decision making
88	Little cooperation from parents
58	Low salary level of teachers

[a]Asked respondents to indicate the three factors that limit the quality of education in Venezuela. There were 11 nonresponses to the question, 19 single-factor responses, and 30 responses with two factors in answer to the question. The cumulative frequency totals represent the number of times a particular factor was indicated by the respondents.

question, as opposed to the two prior questions, may relate to the focus being on current qualitative limits rather than on normative needs and changes.

It is important for educational planners to note that several of the factors that were considered to limit most the quality of education concerned relationships and processes within the system rather than inputs or resources: political partisanship, student-teacher contact, and teacher and student interest (commitment). Some of these factors, while not easy to delimit in problematic terms, represent conditions that can be influenced without utilizing any more resources. The implication is that substantial gains in the quality, and, perhaps, the efficiency, of education may be attained by revitalizing or remanaging the system.

D. Types of Schools (Question 1)

Students were also asked to choose from a list of school levels and types which they felt was most important for Venezuela's needs. The question was: "It is often said that Venezuela does not have enough schools. In your opinion, what two types of schools are most urgently needed?" A ranking of these two responses in table 8 permits some comparisons to be made.

There is a clear concern for expanding technical-vocational schooling at both the university and the secondary levels. This opinion would seem to indicate a practical orientation toward schooling which recognizes both the lack of, and the need for, technicians and vocationally trained workers. Phillip Foster has shown in his Ghana study that students about to enter the labor market are very sensitive to employment opportunities and that the traditional stereotype that the more highly educated shun

TABLE 8[a]

Types of Schools Needed in Venezuela

Type of School	Combined Frequency for First and Second Choice	First Choice (Percentage)
1. University technical institutes	247	19
2. Preschools	199	26
3. Secondary vocational-technical schools	191	16
4. University pedagogic institutes	175	12
5. Primary schools	82	10
6. Academic secondary schools (bachillerato)	74	6
7. Secondary agriculture schools	72	6
8. General university level education	72	3
9. Other categories	30	2

[a]There were sixty-two nonrespondents to this question.

mechanical occupations or training is false (Foster, 1965). It seems, rather, that students will attempt to enter an occupation where they can maximize the probability of succeeding. The question becomes complex as one accounts for the influences of factors that motivate individuals to seek status-roll congruence such as maximum income and social prestige within the constraints of variable market opportunity and of cost sensitivity. Nevertheless, it is important to note that these highly educated and socially successful students value vocational-technical training as an urgent need. While it is not inferred that these students would consider such educational alternatives for themselves (the majority want to work in academic secondary schools), they do seem to value the functional role of schools and they appear concerned with planning priorities in terms of national needs.

The premise above is further substantiated by the relatively infrequent choice of academic secondary schools or universities offering general education as the most critically needed institutions. The nonelitist attitude indicated by these results is consistent with the opinions concerning educational needs already reported.

One noteworthy and unexpected finding showed preschools to be reported by 26 percent (first choice) of all respondents as the type of school most urgently needed. One of the phenomena of an expanding labor market and of modernizing social development may be an increased demand for preschool education, a desire that may reflect both (1) an attitude of granting to schools the responsibility for early childhood socialization and (2) the need for child custodial care thus freeing mothers to accept job opportunities which are increasingly becoming available to them. There is some indication that Venezuela is undergoing both these changes and thus the desire for preschool education may be a result of these recent social and economic developments. The observation in Chapter Two that more highly educated women are more frequently employed raises the question of whether preschooling is demanded just to provide custodial care for working mothers or for other reasons. If one assumes that such mothers are more able to afford domestic help to care for their children, an additional explanation for the priority given preschools by this sample is appropriate. It may be that the students in the sample are familiar with the recent research on child development which suggests that early childhood learning accounts for the majority of the variance in both cognitive and personality development (e.g., Bloom, 1964). A formal environment for learning among the preschool children of the general population of Venezuela, therefore, may be perceived by the sample as being of considerable importance.

Given the averaged importance of preschool education (17 percent combined as opposed to 26 percent first choice), it seems that there were a large number of individuals who stated the need to be paramount, but that the average sentiment across the remaining population was not as concerned with this problem. Only 8 percent of those who did not specify preschool education as their first choice specified it as the second most urgent need.

Analysis of the patterns of response to this question by the independent variable subgroupings yield further insight into the distribution of reported sentiments. Students enrolled at Andrés Bello and Central Universities reported a much higher frequency of concern for preschool education (approximately 55 percent, first choice) than those at other institutions. Only 12 percent of the students enrolled at the Pedagogic Institute of Caracas indicated preschooling as their first concern. There was also a slight upward trend reflecting a greater concern for providing preschool education as the age of the respondents increased. Since employment opportunity increases with age, this phenomenon was to be expected.

In summary, it is observed that the sampled students hold a functional view of education when stating what they see to be the needs for education. When asked to report specific problem areas for education they include process and interaction dimensions of schooling, indicating that the quality of their experience may be enhanced by noncost reforms. Their general belief is that education needs to be expanded, possibly signifying that more opportunity for receiving the benefits of education should be provided.

II. National Development Priorities (Appendix K)

Research relating education and the process of national development indicates that the system of formal education generally subserves dominant political, economic, and social interests. Schools, legitimized and financed as they are by ruling politics, are unable to establish priorities independently of the larger social system. Consequently, the priorities and goals of government and the place that is afforded formal schooling in relation to government objectives is relevant to the present discussion. For this reason two questions were included which asked the sample population for their opinions concerning goals of the Venezuelan government.

A. Goals for National Development (Question 7)

Students were asked the free-response question "what do you feel are the three most critical goals which Venezuela must attend to in fostering national development?" The same analytical procedure used to report the free-response items above-mentioned was employed in this case.[4] Table 9 reports the categorizations made to quantify responses; typical protocols are provided to further define each category.

Table 9 indicates a variation in the ranking of responses on the cumulative versus the first-choice scales. The cumulative frequency figures are considered to be more representative of the sentiment of the total respondent group.

In the opinion of these students the most critical goals for the government to pursue focused principally on education and secondarily upon industrial and economic development. Because the relationship of educational needs to government objectives is an issue of central concern to this study, educational goals were divided into two distinct categores: (1) increasing opportunity, that is, providing more schools, and (2) restructuring the educational system. A predominant concern for expanding education, expressed in responses to other questions, was also reflected here. In addition, students reported a definite, though less frequent, concern for instilling a sense of public social awareness. This attitude seems compatible with the goal of expanding educational opportunity. One could even speculate that the intent of the goal to restructure the educational system was to further democratize schools and create an egalitarian society.

[4]There were 113 nonrespondents to this question and 69 respondents provided incomplete replies. This relatively high level of nonresponse may indicate that the question was stated in such general terms as to be unclear, or that the content of the question is so complex that responses were difficult to make.

63

TABLE 9

Critical Goals for Venezuela's National Development

Goal	Combined Frequency for All Three Responses	First Response (Percentage)
1. Increasing educational opportunity; e.g.: "incremento de la educación"; "educación del mayor número de sus pobladores"; "hacia una educación que llegue a todo el pueblo."	341	34
2. Industrial and economic development; e.g.: "fomentar la industria venezolana"; "creación de nuevas fuentes de trabajo"; "explotación y mejor utilización de recursos naturales."	324	16
3. Increasing a sense of social awareness; e.g.: "hacer tomar conciencia al pueblo de lo importante que es el desarrollo"; "estimular y promover una concientización de todos los habitantes"; "dar mayor cultura a su pueblo."	173	10
4. Restructuring the educational system; e.g.: "mejor desarrollo de la educación"; "creación de escuelas técnicas"; "lograr una reforma total en la educación."	145	13
5. Agricultural development; e.g.: "fomentar nuevos cambios en el desarrollo agrícola"; "la reforma agraria"; "desarrollo de la reforma agraria."	141	6
6. Promoting nationalistic interests; e.g.: "nacionalización del petróleo"; "el nacionalismo"; "independizarse del neo-colonialismo."	132	9
7. Technological development; e.g.: "la tecnificación"; "formación de técnicos en todos los campos"; "abrir los campos más avanzados de tecnología."	111	8
8. Decreasing political intervention; e.g.: "menor presencia de la política"; "no ser tan político"; "reemplazar a los políticos con especialistas en el desarrollo económico."	68	2
9. Other responses	48	2

64

Goals of increasing industrial (economic, agricultural, and technological) development reflect a practical orientation toward providing employment opportunity and economic (personal wealth) growth. The responses grouped as nationalistic interests were most often expressed as an admonition that foreign-owned industry be nationalized and expatriate participation in the Venezuelan economy dissolved. The nationalization of North American industry in Chile by the Allende government only weeks before the sampling, and the political and economic pressure by the Venezuelan government on foreign oil corporations in Venezuela at the same time may have influenced this response.

A subgroup analysis of these responses showed certain group variations. Twice as many men than women mentioned nationalistic interests. This response by men is significantly more frequent than can be expected by chance. Men also responded far more frequently to the seldom used category of political intervention. It was also noted that women expressed a concern for educational goals more frequently than might be expected, though not significantly so.

Subgroup analysis of all these questions turned up only slight variations rather than significant differences for most of the questions. On the question of national goals, for example, both vocational/technical and natural science majors expressed a higher proportionate concern for the development of industry which may reflect an interest in insuring favorable employment opportunities in their own area of specialization. Similarly, students in pedagogy, counseling-administration-evaluation, and academic subject matter specializations expressed a higher proportionate concern for the development of educational opportunities. As stated, however, all variations were slight. The most noteworthy finding of all subgroup analyses performed on these data was that there was random variation in responses across all subgroups and very little variance *between* groups.

It is important to note that there is a range of concern for national objectives among this group of students. Contrary to the popularized stereotypes that often portray university students, particularly Latin Americans, as a homogeneous body of critical radicals whose opinions are quite politicized, these students showed concern for expanding social growth and awareness, building the most underdeveloped areas of the economy, and increasing educational opportunity. In general, their opinions reflect a practical awareness of current social problem areas.

B. Priority Goals of the Venezuelan Government (Question 3)

A companion question to the one above asked which goals "the Venezuelan government regards as most important." This was a forced-choice question for which the sample was requested to make two choices. The intent of the question was to elicit an opinion of goal priorities and governmental commitments. The degree of agreement between the preceding question — which national goals *students* feel are most important — and this question on perceived *government* priorities provides a general estimate of the compatibility or alienation between this student population and the public leadership. The measure of alienation of prospective teachers from the national political structure is important if one assumes that teachers serve as adult role models for students and influence their social values and attitudes.

The response alternatives to this question provided general categories representing broad areas of governmental concern. These categories and the frequencies of response are found in table 10.

TABLE 10

Government Priorities for Venezuela's National Development[a]

Priority	Combined Frequency for First and Second Choices	First Choice (Percentage)
1. Producing more high level, trained manpower	311	28
2. Industrial development, producing more jobs	283	24
3. Expansion of educational opportunities	278	26
4. Social and political unification	139	11
5. Agricultural development, land reform	122	7
6. Other categories	47	4

[a]There were ninety-five nonrespondents to this question.

The patterns of the first and second responses show the results to be fairly consistent. The cumulative rankings placed the production of high-level manpower and industrial development as the perceived top priority objectives of the government, with the expansion of education a close third. Social and political unification, agricultural development, and other goals were clearly perceived as being of less importance to the government.

These results contrast with the rankings of priority goals specified by the respondents as being most important in their own opinion. Education was distinctly the top priority goal in the student ranking, and twice as important as the second goal, industrial and economic development. On the other hand, the government is perceived as promoting high level manpower, a category that, while somewhat related to industrial development, seems to be most closely associated with the seventh-ranked student priority, technological development. One consequence of manpower planning throughout the world has been a concentration upon the training of top-level specialists while relegating to a low priority the educational needs of the masses. The students may be suggesting that they are not satisfied with the extent to which national resources are expended on producing highly trained specialist manpower without providing equal educational opportunity for the majority. Thus, although these students are among the educational elite of the country, they seem to be advocating more opportunity for all rather than the preservation of their exclusive distinction.

Students also placed more importance on the goal of increasing a sense of social awareness than they felt the government placed upon promoting social and political unification. While these two categories seem to represent slightly different connotations, students do seem to feel that this concern is of lesser interest to the government. It is perhaps noteworthy that the categories that were prespecified for this question did not correspond closely with the categories dervied from the responses to the free-response question, an indication of the limitations that must be placed upon interpreting the meaning of forced-choice attitude or opinion surveys. The efforts that have been made in this study to describe and report empirical data will hopefully raise research and policy questions both for educationists and planners.

The results of a later question asking students to list occupations regarded to be most important for development in Venezuela (see Chapter Six) are appropriate to the discussion here. A set of arbitrary occupational categories was created to identify those sectors which students felt were most critically needed for national development. The following areas were reported as being the most urgent: technology (engineer, scientific investigator, laboratory technician) accumulated 579 tallies for the most important, or first priority, sector; teaching (elementary school teacher, secondary school teacher, university professor) tallied 505 responses and was the second most important sector; professional (medical doctor, lawyer) tallied 144 responses; agriculture tallied 131 responses; industry (economist and other nondescript industrial occupations) tallied 129 responses. Thus the overwhelming occupational needs for national development as perceived by this group seems to be focused on the general areas of technological growth and of education.

The results of the question concerning occupational selection tend to reinforce the pervasive concern for expanding educational opportunity and economic growth among members of the sample. The high placement of technology-related jobs and the relatively low placement of industry-related jobs, however, indicates that these students do seem to feel that highly trained specialists are required for overall growth. The means by which such specialists are to be trained continues to pose a challenging question for educational planners and administrators.

Chapter Five
Attitudes Toward Education

A. The Purposes of Education (Appendix L)

As suggested earlier, it is assumed that the attitudes of potential secondary school personnel are important in the national planning and programmatic thrust of education. An understanding of the perceptions of tomorrow's teachers toward their roles in the schools as well as their perception of the schooling process and its potential impact on society are deemed essential to the discovery of what curricular and instructional policies are most likely to gain their confidence and support. As educational priorities are revised, new organizational and administrative programs are implemented, and the instructional process itself undergoes alteration, the attitudes and behaviors of secondary school personnel, especially the teacher, are crucial in terms of increasing the probability of acceptance of changes at the classroom level.

The attitudinal items included in the questionnaire and the sections reporting the results are organized according to four major areas: purposes of education, school's relationship to society, participation in school management and decision making, and responsibility for student learning.

1) *Educational philosophy (Question 81).* The series of questions directed toward assessing the sample's attitudes toward the general purposes of education were based upon four factors or orientations and attempted to place the respondent in situations where he would have to favor one factor or orientation over another. The four orientations were: education as preparation for an occupational future, education for the scholarly pursuit of knowledge and the cultivation of the intellect, education as a means of reaching the objectives and needs of the greater society, and education geared to individualistic interests and styles as well as to a concern for personal identity.

These four personal philosophies of education were briefly described in the questionnaire and students were asked to order hierarchically the four descriptions in accord with the way in which each portrayed his own point of view. The question reads as follows:

> Students hold a variety of attitudes about their own educational purposes and goals. Below are descriptive statements of four such "personal philosophies" which there is reason to believe are quite prevalent. As you read the four statements, attempt to determine how close each comes to your own philosophy of education.

> PHILOSOPHY A: This philosophy emphasizes education essentially as preparation for an *occupational future*. Social or purely intellectual phases of life are relatively less important.

> PHILOSOPHY B: This philosophy, while it does not ignore career preparation, assigns greatest importance to the *scholarly pursuit of knowledge*. It attaches greatest importance to interest in ideas and to the cultivation of the intellect.

> PHILOSOPHY C: This philosophy emphasizes the *objectives and needs of the greater society*. The individual is seen as a contributor to national growth and development rather than as one who works independently for his own personal future.

> PHILOSOPHY D: This philosophy emphasizes *individualistic interests* and styles and concern for personal identity. Traditionally held value orientations or aspirations of the society at large are relatively less important.

> Rank the accuracy with which each philosophy portrays *your own* point of view. (Place (1) by the philosophy *most* descriptive of your views, (2) by the next most descriptive, then (3), and (4) by that which least describes your personal views).

The results showed solid support for viewing education as a means of reaching the objectives and needs of society. Viewing the responses of the sample only by the philosophy accorded the highest priority, 55 percent indicated their preference for societal objectives and needs. In second and third places the preferences were equally divided between education for an occupational future and education for the scholarly pursuit of knowledge. The last preference, individualistic interests and personal identity was clearly accorded the lowest priority as 72 percent of the sample reported it was of least importance of the four possible responses.

Students at Central and Los Andes Universities, as well as majors in humanities, physical education, and commerce tended to rate societal objectives and needs as of lesser importance. A percentage of affirmative preferences slightly higher than the norm was recorded by students at the Pedagogic Institute of Barquisimeto for education as preparation for an occupational future, while students at the University of the Andes tended to see this preference as of less importance. Counseling-evaluation-administration majors also viewed occupational futures as less important than the norm while students majoring in technical-vocational, physical education, and commerce viewed education as occupational preparation more positively than the norm. Students enrolled in the first year, as opposed to those in the last, were inclined to view preparation for an occupation more favorably. Students at the two pedagogic institutes, and those majoring in language and physical science, were more favorably disposed toward the scholarly pursuit of knowledge orientation than the respective norms, whereas technical-vocational and physical education majors were more negatively disposed to this preference. More negative appraisals of the philosophy oriented toward individual interests and personal identy were reported from Andrés Bello and Central Universities and from the Pedagogic Institute at Barquisimeto. There was a tendency for students to view education for individual interests and personal identity more positively as they progressed through their respective institutions.

To assess the reliability of student responses in terms of their perceptions of the purposes of education, major components of the four philosophies were placed one against the other in a series of questionnaire statements. Students were instructed to indicate whether they agreed or disagreed with the statements on a four-point scale. As with all attitudinal questions, a multivariate analysis was used to test for differences among respondents according to the student's institutional affiliation, age, sex, year-in-school, major, and the level of education achieved by his parents. Significant differences were found among the sex, year-in-school, and major field of study categories.

71

The eight statements used to assess the reliability of the respondents' perception of the purposes of education emphasized the development of the intellect, preparation for an occupation, cultivation of the individual, and social needs and objectives. Each statement posed two purposes, emphasizing the importance of one over another, and the eight statements included all possible combinations. Table 11 lists the eight statements and reports the means for each of the four response categories; tables 16, 17, 18 report the results of all multivariate analyses by sex, major, and year in school.

2) *Intellectual development and occupational training (Questions 22, 84)*. The first of the eight statements read as follows: "Schools should emphasize the development of the intellect rather than the development of occupational skills." On a four-point agree-disagree scale 62 percent of the sample disagreed with the statement. When the first- and second-year student responses were compared with those of the third-, fourth-, and fifth-year students, a significant difference (> 0.0004) in favor of the lower classmen was noted indicating more agreement with the statement by the first- and second-year students. A similar statement, this one emphasizing a sound academic background over occupational training found 72 percent in disagreement but no significant differences between groups.

3) *Intellectual development, personal identity, and occupational training (Questions 26, 92)*. A third statement emphasized the development of the intellect over the school's role in contributing to a student's personal identity. Once again, general disagreement was registered, with 80 percent indicating that they could not support the idea that it was more important to develop the intellect of students than, in this case, to contribute to their personal identity. A difference, however, in the response pattern among students according to major field of study occurred (> 0.01). Students enrolled in pedagogy and counseling-administration-evaluation perceived the statement the most negatively while humanities and language majors perceived the statement the most positively. The remaining fields of study were found between these other groupings. Reversing the statement in another section of the questionnaire, an opposite response pattern

72

TABLE 11

Educational Philosophy

Questionnaire Number	Statement	Mean	Standard Deviation	(In Percentages)			
				Strongly Agree	Agree	Disagree	Strongly Disagree
22	Schools should emphasize the development of the intellect rather than the development of occupational skills.	2.346	0.913	13	25	45	62
84	It is more important for the schools to provide a sound academic background than to provide occupational training.	2.231	0.765	8	20	60	13
26	It is more important for schools to develop the intellect of students than to contribute to their personal identity.	1.971	0.797	5	15	52	28
92	The emotional and personal development of a student should be as important to a teacher as his intellectual development.	3.440	0.597	48	49	2	1
95	Schools should be concerned with providing individuals with the knowledge to solve pressing social problems rather than with training them for specific jobs.	2.782	0.792	18	47	30	5
96	Schools should teach knowledge and truth rather than being concerned with social values and norms.	2.629	0.842	18	33	43	6
97	Schools should be guided more by the individual interests of students than by the welfare of the society at large.	1.997	0.739	5	14	59	23
111	Subject matter in school should relate less to training students for jobs and relate more to the cultivation of the individual.	2.524	0.805	11	39	42	9

73

among students was apparent although no statistically significant differences among groups were noted. The statement read: "The emotional and personal development of a student should be as important to a teacher as his intellectual development." Ninety-seven percent of the sample agreed.

4) *Intellectual development, social issues, and occupational training (Questions 95, 96, 97, 111).* The fifth entry stated that "schools should be more concerned with providing individuals with the knowledge to solve social problems than with training them for specific jobs." The respondents were generally in favor of the statement with 65 percent in agreement. Male and female respondents differed significantly (> 0.03) in their reactions to this statement with males agreeing more strongly than females that knowledge for solving social problems is more important than job training.

Students were divided (51 percent in agreement) over a statement that the school's major concerns should place "knowledge and truth" over "social values and norms."

When asked to agree or disagree that the school "should be guided more by the individual interests of students than by the welfare of the society at large," 82 percent of the sample disagreed. Students enrolled in their third, fourth, or fifth year of studies were in significantly (> 0.01) less disagreement with the statement than students enrolled in their first or second year of studies. Finally, students were divided in their response to the statement that curricular content should be related more to the cultivation of the individual than to job training.

The responses to these eight statements generally supported the response to the broader "personal philosophies" question reported above. It ill be remembered that the majority of the students (55 percent) ranked the needs and objectives of society as most important in response to that question. In the separate statements, the students generally rejected an intellectual or academic educational orientation when it was placed against occupational and personal orientations but accepted knowledge to solve social problems when placed against occupation. The sample was divided in its response to knowledge and truth when included with social values and norms. Thus, one might conclude that the sample was generally anti-intellectual when it came to knowledge for its own

74

sake, and was generally pro-intellectual if knowledge was pragmatic and utilitarian. The students also indicated that they were more likely to be concerned with the collective welfare of society than with the individual interests of members of that society and were equally divided when asked to choose between occupational training and the cultivation of the individual.

5) *Objectives of the secondary school (Question 2).* In a somewhat more direct and forthright approach to the purposes of education, a multiple-choice response question was used to assess what the sample felt the principal objectives of the school for youth twelve to eighteen years of age should be. The choices were university preparation, civic responsibility, the improvement of character, general culture, occupational preparation, and a capacity to reason. The respondents were asked to give their first and second choices. The overall results of the combined choices indicated that "to prepare students for an occupation" was ranked first, followed by general culture, university preparation, and civic responsibility. The older students in the sample were more likely to mark occupational preparation whereas the younger students in the sample were more likely to mark general culture. Similarly, students enrolled in their later years of schooling were likely to mark occupational preparation, while students in their early years tended to rank civic responsibility as important. As the level of education achieved by the parents increased, it was more likely that students of these parents would consider choices other than occupational preparation as important.

The responses here tend to be at odds with the prior questions if one interprets general culture as the cultivation of the individual, university preparation as intellectual formation, and civic responsibility as needs and objectives of society. It might be assumed that since this question directed attention toward students of secondary school age whereas the former questions referred to teachers, schools, or education in general, the sample was inclined to recognize Venezuela's need for middle-level technical and skilled manpower and thus altered considerably their orientation toward the role of schools generally. These distinct response patterns suggest that considerable importance should be given not only to the format for inquiry into attitudes but to the specific level of schooling involved, since in this case

75

the general orientation to education was distinct from an orientation toward the function of secondary schools.

Before turning to the policy implications of these response patterns it is necessary to turn to some additional inquiries into the factors affecting occupational training, fostering individuality, and addressing social problems included in the eight statements. These additional statements required agree-disagree responses (table 12).

6) *Occupational training (Questions 82, 93).* The sample was asked to respond to two statements on occupational training: (1) schools should be used to train individuals for jobs and (2) students should be permitted to earn school credit by working in a factory or as an apprentice learning a skill. Both statements found the sample in strong agreement, with 83 percent concurring with the first and 86 percent concurring with the second. First- and second-year students, when compared with third-, fourth-, and fifth-year students, differed significantly (> 0.006) in favor of the upper classmen with regard to students being able to secure school credit for learning a skill outside of school. One may hypothesize, therefore, that as students progress through school they tend to see a greater need for sharing the educational responsibility with other social institutions. This orientation showed up earlier when the sample disagreed with the statement "schools should emphasize the development of the intellect rather than the development of occupational skills," with lower classmen expressing significantly more agreement with the statement than upper classmen.

7) *Individuality and freedom (Questions 15, 25, 18).* A second factor for additional inquiry was the area of individuality and freedom for students. The statement, "Schools should emphasize student freedom, initiative, and creativity" found 98 percent of the sample in agreement, 70 percent of them in strong agreement. Statistically significant differences were noted among sex (> 0.01) and year-in-school (> 0.03) categories with males and third-, fourth-, and fifth-year students in greater agreement with the statement than females and students in their first two years.

Students also agreed (92 percent) with the statement "Secondary school teachers should encourage students to pursue their own individual interests." When the sample was confronted with the

76

TABLE 12

Occupational Training, Individuality, Social Problems

Questionnaire Number	Statement	Mean	Standard Deviation	(In Percentages)			
				Strongly Agree	Agree	Disagree	Strongly Disagree
82	Schools should be used to train individuals for jobs.	3.088	0.720	28	54	15	2
93	Secondary school students should be allowed to earn school credit by working in a factory or as an apprentice learning a skill.	3.137	0.690	30	57	12	2
15	Schools should emphasize student freedom, initiative, and creativity.	3.673	0.530	70	28	2	1
25	Secondary school teachers should encourage students to pursue their own individual interests.	3.336	0.690	44	48	6	2
18	Schools should permit students to establish their own individualized program of study rather than providing an established curriculum.	2.505	0.923	17	29	41	13
23	Secondary school teachers should relate the content of their courses to current social problems.	3.482	0.650	55	40	3	2
91	School is equal to life and real life problems must be emphasized in school.	2.900	0.747	20	54	22	4
27	Controversial issues should be discussed in the classroom.	3.089	0.796	33	47	17	4
89	Social values are relative to a given time and place and must be continually questioned.	2.914	0.768	21	54	20	5
83	Secondary school teachers should encourage students to question and examine social values.	3.315	0.657	38	56	5	1

statement that students should be permitted to plan their own individualized program of study rather than adhere to an already established one, however, 54 percent of the sample disagreed. A statistically significant (> 0.0001) difference was noted among the students by major field of study with pedagogy and counseling-administration-evaluation majors agreeing more than humanities and language majors, and both groups agreeing more than the remaining majors.

The results here suggest that although prospective secondary school personnel are close to unanimity in terms of sanctioning freedom, initiative, and creativity on the part of students, they are not yet ready to relinquish their control over the establishment of the curriculum to which students should be exposed. Thus, when asked generally about the notion of student freedom, initiative and creativity they overwhelmingly concur but when queried on a specific aspect of traditional school policy which might accomplish these objectives, they chose to accept instead the traditional policy.

8) *Social problems and issues (Questions 23, 91, 27, 89,83).* The last factor explored in regard to the purposes of education was the area of social problems and issues. The five statements included in this section attempted to clarify the position of the school and the teacher in promoting socially relevant experiences for students.

The first statement suggested that "secondary school teachers should relate the content of their courses to current social problems." Ninety-five percent of the sample agreed. A significant difference (> 0.03) appeared among major fields of specialization with pedagogy and counseling-evaluation-administration majors in most agreement, followed by humanities and language and then all remaining majors. Seventy-four percent of the sample concurred with the statement, "School is equal to life and real life problems must be emphasized in school." The results indicated that males were significantly (> 0.04) in more agreement in their responses than females. The third statement attempted to assess whether or not the sample would view controversial issues as appropriate subject matter for classroom discussion. Eighty percent of the sample was in agreement and significant differences emerged among majors and between sexes.[1] Pedagogy and counseling-administration-evaluation majors agreed with the statement more than did humanities and language majors, and both groups were in more agreement than other majors (>0.001). Males agreed significantly (>0.007) more than females. The last two statements were concerned with the area of values and assessed the respondent's orientation to continually analyzing such values in the context of schooling. The statement, "Social values are relative to a given time and place and must be continually questioned" was agreed with by 75 percent of the sample with males in significantly (>0.005) more agreement than females. The final statement that "teachers should encourage students to question and examine social values" produced results indicating that 94 percent of the sample agreed.

One may conclude that the sample is very positively oriented in terms of their attitudes toward directing the schooling process to confront social problems and issues. Males tend to be in stronger agreement with this orientation than females and pedagogy and counseling-administration-evaluation majors were more positive than humanities and language majors, who in turn were more favorable than the remaining majors.

Summary and conclusions. Several conclusions may be drawn from the responses of the sample to the questions and statements pertaining to attitudes toward education. Regarding the purposes of education, occupational preparation at the secondary school level and meeting the needs and objectives of the society for education in general were the apparent trends in the data. These results suggest a rather pragmatic orientation, one in which intellectual values are of lesser importance. It can be hypothesized that prospective secondary school personnel are open to the priorities of national development planning and are willing to expend energy and devote themselves to meeting such ends through their potential activities in the school and classroom. For

---

[1] Albornoz (1965) found that 54 percent of his sample of primary school teachers thought that sex education should be taught at all levels of the primary school while Gross et al. (1968 reported 85 percent of their sample thought that sex education (and religious instruction) should definitely or probably be the responsibility of the school.

example, the students seem to be ready for some experimentation with educational alternatives since they were close to unanimity in their feeling that students should be permitted to earn school credit while working on the job in apprenticeship positions in industry. They are less clear, however, in their willingness to permit students to plan their own courses of study even though 46 percent of the sample are in agreement. The students are in favor of involving themselves with social, even controversial, issues in the classroom, thus bringing into the school activities that concern real life problems.

Males tend to be more liberal than females in their orientations to these areas. When significant differences did occur by sex, males were in more agreement than females with statements that would apply knowledge to solving social problems, bring real life problems into the school, bring controversial issues into the classroom, and question social values. Males also tended to be more favorably disposed toward schools encouraging student freedom, initiative, and creativity.

Students enrolled in their third, fourth, or fifth year of studies tended to be more liberal than students in their first two years of study. They were generally more inclined to favor occupational training, to favor promoting individual interests of students, to permit students to earn credits for work in industry, and to value student freedom, initiative, and creativity. These significant differences among students by year-in-school are probably related to the fact that the advanced students were more likely to be returning to the university after some experience in schools and because of their increased training were more aware of, and more inclined to take a stand on, the issues that they know are confronting Venezuela and its educational system. Pedagogy and counseling-administration-evaluation majors were generally more favorable in their orientation toward these same issues than humanities and language majors, who, in turn, were more inclined than other majors to be in agreement. These results indicated that this ordering by major was true for more favorable perceptions toward statements that suggested that students should be permitted to develop their own course of study, that classroom content should be directed toward social problems, and that controversial issues should be discussed in the classroom. Pedagogy and counseling-administration-evaluation majors were also the most negative toward a statement that suggested that intellectual goals should be given more weight in the educational system than goals that concern personal identity.

Thus, one can suggest that in terms of this sample, prospective secondary school personnel are a relatively flexible population with whom change and innovation are feasible. Males and pedagogy-administration-evaluation majors are the most flexible in this regard. Students who are in their later years of study are likewise more liberally oriented. It should be noted that pedagogy and counseling-administration-evaluation majors were found only in Central, Andrés Bello, and Los Andes Universities. These majors constituted the only third-year students in the sample although some individuals majoring in these areas were enrolled in the second and fourth year of studies as well.

B. The School's Relationship to Society (Appendix M)

There were thirteen agree-disagree statements assessing the school's relationship to society. The content of these statements addressed the issues of educational relevance, social class differences in terms of access to schooling, and parental and community involvement in the educational process (table 13).

1) *Educational relevance (Questions 34, 104, 101).* The first statement read as follows: "In general the overall curriculum taught in secondary school is relevant and useful to national development in Venezuela." The results indicated that 83 percent of the sample disagreed with the statement, with males significantly (> 0.004) more in disagreement than females. In response to a similar statement, "Secondary schools are providing students with the knowledge, attitudes and values which are relevant to their future lives," 59 percent of the sample was in agreement. This stark contrast between the two very likely rests with the wording of the statements. The sample disagreed when the statement suggested curricular relevance for national development, whereas the sample agreed when the statement suggested school relevance for an individual's future. This clearly important distinction indicates that the sample is perhaps suggesting that schools are currently relevant to the status quo but that the curriculum is not attuned to the needs and objectives of a rapidly

81

TABLE 13

The School's Relationship to Society

Questionnaire Number	Statement	Mean	Standard Deviation	(In Percentages)			
				Strongly Agree	Agree	Disagree	Strongly Disagree
34	In general, the overall curriculum taught in secondary school is relevant and useful to national development in Venezuela.	1.878	0.730	2	15	52	31
104	Secondary schools are providing students with the knowledge, attitudes and values which are relevant to their future lives.	2.636	0.804	13	46	33	8
101	Schools can change society by instilling appropriate attitudes and values in students.	3.081	0.722	27	57	12	3
24	Students are influenced *more* by what they learn outside of school than by what they learn in school.	2.527	0.827	13	36	43	9
33	Students who remain in school become better citizens than those who drop out of school.	2.598	0.927	19	33	36	12
85	Citizenship training should be done by the community and the family, not the school.	2.243	0.801	9	21	56	14
30	The student learns discipline for adult life by listening to adults.	2.314	0.799	6	33	46	15
102	Most Venezuelan parents are capable of teaching their children about life in a modern society.	2.215	0.795	8	22	55	16
36	A secondary school education is a privilege rather than a right.	1.861	0.889	7	13	39	41
88	As a highly educated minority, secondary school graduates have every right to expect jobs which do not require physical work.	2.287	0.756	7	28	54	12
109	Middle and upper class families prepare their children to achieve at a higher level in school than do lower class families.	2.276	0.900	11	26	43	20
35	The school is society's way of separating the rich from the poor.	1.785	0.793	5	9	47	40
86	Secondary schools are designed to serve the students from middle and upper class families rather than from lower class families.	2.111	0.882	9	18	49	25

changing society. The potential for the school to be a resource for national development is apparently accepted by the sample as 85 percent agreed that "Schools can change society by instilling appropriate attitudes and values in students." The previous responses suggest, however, that the student sample feels that currently this change is not occurring to the extent it should.

2) *Parental and community involvement (Questions 24, 33, 85, 30, 102)*. The next group of statements was addressed to whether the family and community or the school were best equipped to teach children.

In response to the statement "Students are influenced *more* by what they learn outside of school than by what they learn in school" the sample was divided, with 51 percent in disagreement. Males differed significantly (> 0.01) from females with the former in greater agreement than the latter, and third-, fourth-, and fifth-year students were significantly (> 0.002) in more agreement than first- and second-year students. A significant (> 0.01) difference also occurred among majors with pedagogy and counseling-administration-evaluation majors in more agreement than humanities and language majors, and both of the above groups were in more agreement with the statement than the remaining majors. This response suggests a somewhat idealistic orientation toward the impact of the school since considerable literature indicates that social and economic surroundings, especially during the early childhood years, have an overwhelming impact on the formation of the individual both cognitively and emotionally. (see, e.g., Bloom, 1964.) This orientation toward the school's impact tends to be supported by the sample's response to the statement, "Students who remain in school become better citizens than those who drop out of school." The results indicated that 53 percent of the sample agreed. Similarly, 70 percent of the sample disagreed that "citizenship training should be done by the community and the family, not the school."

At least half of the prospective secondary school personnel sampled seems to be convinced that schools not only make a difference to the future of an individual and to the future of society, but a higher percentage also seem to feel that schools may be the only institution that can do justice to the teaching-learning process relating to citizenship training. Two additional statements were presented to the sample to further test such orientations. One statement suggested that "students learn discipline for adult life by listening to adults," and the other that "most Venezuelan parents are capable of teaching their children about life in a modern society." Sixty percent of the sample disagreed with the first statement, with a significant (> 0.02) difference evident among majors. Pedagogy and counseling-administration-evaluation majors disagreed the most, followed by humanities and language majors, and then by the remaining majors. Seventy-one percent disagreed with the second statement concerning the capabilities of Venezuelan parents.

These last two responses tend to support attitudes expressed earlier. The sample is generally liberal in its orientation to student freedom and initiative and thus one may suspect that the instructional process as perceived by the sample is not of the teacher-lecturer variety so that listening to adults is not the most appropriate mode of learning. This orientation does not detract, however, from the general institutional bias evident in the responses of the sample. Ideal learning may not occur by listening to adults, but such learning, according to the sample, apparently does occur primarily inside schools or other formal institutions rather than under the auspices of parents or members of the community.

3) *Social class backgrounds and access to schools (Questions 36, 88, 109, 35, 86).* The third area of investigation regarding the school's relationship to society concerned access to schools with special emphasis on the social class backgrounds of students. The recent empirical literature (Coleman, 1966; Central Advisory Council on Education, 1966) as well as the writing of scholars and critics (Illich, 1970) suggests that the social class background of students is a primary casual factor in student achievement and also indicates that schools in developing countries serve primarily children from middle and upper class families rather than children from lower class families. Thus, although some research shows some mobility for lower class youngsters in secondary school attendance (Havighurst and Gouveia, 1969) it has long been known that lower class youngsters predominate among dropouts and repeaters at the elementary school level and are relatively seldom found at the secondary school level.

The first statement in this area read: "A secondary education is a privilege rather than a right." The responses found 80 percent of the sample in disagreement with a significant (> 0.04) difference noted among students by year-in-school. Third-, fourth-, and fifth-year students disagreed with the statement more than first- and second-year students. A second statement, "As a highly educated minority, secondary school graduates have every right to expect jobs which do not require physical work," found 66 percent of the sample in disagreement. The responses to these inquiries generally support the attitudinal responses reported earlier, that is, a rather liberal or open orientation to the needs of society and to the importance of occupational preparation. In this case the sample found secondary education a right rather than a privilege and seemed to feel that graduates should be prepared to engage in physical work. It may support the student's bias toward post-secondary school technical institutes reported in the preceding chapter.

Three additional statements, these concerning the social class backgrounds of students, were also included in this section. The first read as follows: "Middle and upper class families prepare their children to achieve at a higher level in school than do lower class families." The sample was divided on this statement with 51 percent in agreement. Thus, one might assume that more than half the students are aware of the rather well-established statistical data regarding the influence of social class on student achievement.

Regarding the points made by Illich and others, however, the sample was in general disagreement. To the statement, "The school is society's way of separating the rich from the poor," 86 percent disagreed. To the statement, "Secondary schools are designed to serve the students from middle and upper class families rather than from lower class families," 73 percent of the sample disagreed with females significantly (> 0.003) more in disagreement than males. One may assume, on the basis of these responses, that the sample clearly perceives schools as serving equally all social classes. Such a pattern of response may well be due to the mobility achieved by many of the respondents themselves. Although we were unable to secure social class indicators from the sample to test this assumption, it is known that a small minority of the students had parents who had graduated from secondary schools or had post-secondary school exposure. On this basis one might hypothesize that these statements were generally alien to the student's own personal experiences since they themselves had exceeded the level of education achieved by their parents.

Summary and conclusions. The sample's general orientation to the role of schools in society revealed, first, that although it perceives schools as being capable of changing society by instilling attitudes and values in students, it does not find the current curriculum appropriate to this end. Instead the students responding indicated that currently the experiences encountered in school are appropriate for individual needs but not for the needs of a developing society. Second, the sample generally perceived the role of the schools in the education process as more important than the role of parents and the community. This institutional bias in favor of schools, if widespread, may not auger well for the establishment of alternatives to schools if the alternatives imply placing a heavier load on parents and the community. On the other hand, responses to an earlier statement suggesting the granting of school credit for pursuing on-the-job training, indicated general acceptance, suggesting perhaps that if alternatives to schools were to be fostered they would be more acceptable to secondary school personnel if they were planned instructional programs carried out inside institutions through which students could earn school credits.

Third, the sample was generally agreed that secondary education is a right rather than a privilege and that secondary school graduates should not consider themselves an elitist minority unable to engage in physical work. Furthermore, although the sample was divided as to whether middle and upper class parents prepared their children to achieve at a higher level in school than lower class parents, the responses did indicate substantial disagreement that the secondary school was designed to better serve the needs of middle and upper class families than those of lower class families. This disagreement may have stemmed from the student's own background and experience, for the majority of the respondents came from other than middle or upper class families, thus they responded to the statements as persons served well by secondary schools rather than as persons alienated by such schools.

The general trend already established in the significant differences occurring among the various groups appeared to hold. Males tended to be both more critical and more liberal than females; more males than females disagreed that the secondary school curriculum was relevant to national development in Venezuela; males agreed more strongly that students are influenced more by what they learn outside of school; and they registered more agreement that secondary schools are designed to serve the students from middle and upper class families. Among students grouped according to fields of specialization, pedagogy and counseling-administration-evaluation majors were more critical and liberal than humanities and language majors, and both former groups were more so oriented than the latter majors. The same ranking was apparent in agreeing that students are influenced more by what they learn outside of school and in disagreeing that the student learns discipline for adult life by listening to adults. More first- and second-year students agreed that secondary education was a privilege rather than a right; and more third-, fourth-, and fifth-year students agreed that students are influenced more by what they learn outside of school rather than by what they learn in school.

C. School Management and Participation in Decision Making (Appendix N)

A series of attitude statements was directed toward uncovering the perceptions of students toward the management of schooling focusing on the participation of government, teachers, students, and parents in the decision-making process (see table 14 for results).

1) *Administrator-Teacher involvement (Questions 29, 98, 57, 110).* In Chapter Three on professional expectations it was reported that 68 percent of the sample indicated that they would expect to have the liberty to express their opinion on involvement in the administration of the school in which they were working. Thirty-six percent indicated that an official from the Ministry of Education would pay little attention to a teacher's opinion if that teacher felt that a ministerial ruling would prove harmful to education in Venezuela. In addition, it was reported that 54

TABLE 14

School Management and Participation in Decision Making

(In Percentages)

Questionnaire Number	Statement	Mean	Standard Deviation	Strongly Agree	Agree	Disagree	Strongly Disagree
29	A strong central government is the best way to avoid inefficiency in Venezuela's educational system.	2.672	0.903	19	41	29	11
98	Teachers should have considerably more to say about how schools operate.	3.455	0.521	47	53	1	1
110	If controversial issues are discussed in the classroom, the teacher, as civil servant, should be permitted to express personal opinions.	3.121	0.728	30	55	12	3
108	Pupils should participate in establishing the policies of a secondary school.	2.533	0.861	11	44	32	13
103	Secondary school teachers should invite students to help make class plans or policy.	2.975	0.750	23	56	17	4
21	Secondary school teachers should invite students to criticize their ideas.	3.312	0.754	46	44	8	3
90	Although many students are clamoring for new freedoms, few are capable of using those freedoms responsibly.	2.987	0.759	23	57	15	5
99	Parents should be expected to aid the school in educating their children.	3.507	0.586	55	43	2	1
107	Final decisions about education should be made by professional educators rather than by parents.	2.561	0.858	16	37	39	10

percent would actually try to influence a ministerial official if such a ruling was being contemplated. A related statement concerning government involvement in education is reported here. The statement read "A strong central government is the best way to avoid inefficiency in Venezuela's educational system." Sixty percent of the sampled concurred. Females were in significantly (> 0.02) more agreement with the statement than males and first- and second-year students were in significantly (> 0.0008) more agreement with the statement than third-, fourth-, and fifth-year students.

Central government involvement apparently does not mean, however, that teachers should not participate in the formulation of school policy. When the sample was presented the following statement, "Teachers should have considerably more to say about how schools operate," 99 percent agreed.

In an attempt to reconcile somewhat the question of centralized versus decentralized authority, two items relating to the teaching of controversial issues were included. The first was a question, the results of which were reported in Chapter Three, and was posed in the following manner, "Suppose you were asked to teach material which contradicted some of your own values and beliefs; what would you do?" About 41 percent of the sample replied that they would teach the material but present their own point of view. The other inquiry in this regard was an agree-disagree statement and read, "If controversial issues are discussed in the classroom, the teacher, as a civil servant, should be permitted to express personal opinions." Eighty-five percent of the sample agreed.

This series of items leaves an unclear impression as to the perception of secondary school personnel regarding the role of the government versus the teacher in the operation of schools. It can be assumed that the sample is generally agreed that for purposes of efficiency a centralized government is most advantageous. At the same time, the responses of the sample indicate that "teachers should have considerably more to say about how schools operate." The two responses may refer to distinct areas of decision making as perceived by the students. When a somewhat less obtrusive approach to this area of inquiry is used, centering on the teaching of controversial issues, the sample generally concurred that they would teach material that contradicted their own values if asked to do so, but at the same time they would not hesitate to express personal opinions or their own point of view.

2) *Student involvement (Questions 108, 103, 21, 90).* A second series of statements on school management concerns the involvement of students in the operation of schools. The first statement read, "Pupils should participate in establishing the policies of a secondary school." About 55 percent of the sample agreed with the statement with a significant difference (> 0.02) occurring among students according to year-in-school. Third-, fourth-, and fifth-year students were more in agreement with the statement than first- and second-year students. Considerably more agreement, 79 percent was registered in response to the statement, "Secondary school teachers should invite students to help make class plans or policy." Pedagogy and counseling-administration-evaluation majors registered more agreement than humanities and language majors, and both groups were more in favor than the remaining majors (>0.0004). Even stronger agreement was recorded in terms of the statement, "Secondary school teachers should invite students to criticize their ideas." In this instance 89 percent of the sample marked either strongly agree or agree and significant differences occurred by sex (> 0.002) and major (> 0.01). Males agreed more than females and pedagogy and counseling-administration-evaluation majors more than either humanities and language or remaining majors.

Thus, one may assume that secondary school personnel are inclined to invite students both to assist in the development of class plans and policy and to criticize the secondary school teacher's ideas. The sample is not as strongly agreed, however, that students should participate in the establishment of secondary school policies.

An additional statement, this one designed to further assess the area of student involvement, read as follows: "Although many students are clamoring for new freedoms, few are capable of using those freedoms responsibly." Eighty percent agreed with significant differences occurring among students in accord with year-in-school (> 0.01) and major fields of specialization (> 0.03) categories. More third-, fourth-, and fifth-year students agreed with the statement than did first- and second-year students, while humanities and language majors agreed with the statement, the most and pedagogy and counseling-administration-evaluation majors disagreed with it the most.

3) *Parental involvement (Questions 99, 107).* The final set of questions on school management included two related to the involvement of parents. One statement, "Parents should be expected to aid the school in educating their children," found general agreement by 97 percent of the sample. To the second statement, "Final decisions about education should be made by professional educators rather than by parents," however, only 51 percent of the sample was in agreement.

Summary and conclusions. Although the questions regarding school policy and decision making are lacking both in breadth and depth of inquiry, several tentative statements may be made regarding some apparent trends. First, the sample sees a combination of centralized and decentralized policies for the operation of the schools. Although they envision a major role for teachers in the operation, they do not negate the importance of having a strong central government manage the educational bureaucracy. In terms of student involvement, generally the sample appears eager to have students assume a critically active role in the instructional process at the classroom level. On the other hand, 55 percent of the sample felt that students should be involved in the establishment of secondary school policies. Furthermore, the sample clearly agreed that although "students are clamoring for new freedoms, few are capable of using those freedoms responsibly." The sample was highly supportive of parental participation in the school's educational functions. At the same time, the sample was generally divided over whether professional educators or parents should be vested with the power and responsibility of making final decisions about education.

Males were significantly more in favor of teachers inviting students to criticize their ideas than females, while males and students enrolled in their last three years of school were in less agreement than their respective counterparts with the notion that a strong central government is the best way to avoid inefficiency in Venezuela's educational system. Upper classmen were also in more agreement than lower classmen that pupils should participate in the establishment of secondary school policy and similarly that few students are capable of using new found freedoms responsibly. Among majors, pedagogy and counseling-administration-evaluation students were in more agreement than either humanities and language majors and, in turn, than the remaining majors, that teachers should invite students to help make class plans or policy and that teachers should invite students to criticize their ideas. On the other hand, humanities and language majors were in most agreement and pedagogy and counseling-administration-evaluation majors were in least agreement, that "although many students are clamoring for new freedoms, few are capable of using those freedoms responsibly."

D. Responsibility for Student Learning (Appendix O)

The final section of this chapter concerns the attitudes of the sample toward learning, with special emphasis on teacher behavior and responsibility (see table 15). More specifically, the results of the agree-disagree statements reported here concern student and teacher responsibility for student learning, the involvement of teachers with students in the learning process, and the climate under which learning occurs.

1) *Teacher-student responsibility (Questions 100, 31, 112, 106, 87).* On the question of responsibility for student learning, 54 percent of the sample disagreed that "The teacher should decide what knowledge the child is to learn." Although the responses to this question were generally divided between students who agreed and disagreed, the results appear to substantiate a trend based on prior responses on management and decision making where there was general agreement that teachers should solicit student assistance in classroom plans and policy, and that teachers should invite students to criticize their ideas. Furthermore, the sample was almost evenly divided in response to the statement, "Final decisions about education should be made by professional educators rather than by parents" (see table 14). The fact that the student sample registered some disagreement with the idea that teachers should decide what the child is to learn while at the same time indicating that parents and

TABLE 15

Responsibility for Student Learning

Questionnaire Number	Statement	Mean	Standard Deviation	Strongly Agree	Agree	Disagree	Strongly Disagree
				(In Percentages)			
100	The teacher should decide what knowledge the child is to learn.	2.438	0.889	12	34	39	15
31	When a student fails in school, only he is to blame.	1.743	0.767	4	5	53	38
112	When a student fails in school, the teacher must accept responsibility for his failure.	2.925	0.813	24	50	20	6
106	All a teacher can do is present the material, it is up to the student to learn.	1.893	0.791	5	10	53	32
87	The classroom performance of a student should be evaluated in relation to his capacities.	2.931	0.831	26	47	22	6
32	A teacher can be effective without personally involving himself with his students.	2.205	0.868	9	22	48	20
105	It is a teacher's responsibility to help students with personal problems they may have.	3.026	0.711	24	58	16	3
20	Schools cannot be fun since students must work in order to learn anything worthwhile.	1.788	0.784	4	9	47	39
17	Secondary school teachers should try to present materials in an entertaining way.	3.377	0.766	52	38	7	4
28	Teachers should act so as to reduce the excessively competitive nature of the school system and to promote a spirit of cooperation and group effort.	3.423	0.676	51	44	3	2
94	Student freedoms should be limited in the interest of learning.	2.453	0.809	11	34	46	10
16	Without tests and grades to prod them, most students would learn little.	2.602	0.927	18	37	33	13

students should be involved can, therefore, be interpreted as an orientation toward sharing that responsibility with parents, students, and very likely officials at the ministerial level.

In an attempt to further delimit teacher as opposed to student responsibility, two statements concerning student failure and two statements concerning student learning were presented to the sample. Ninety-one percent disagreed that "when a student fails in school, only he is to blame." First- and second-year students agreed with the statement significantly (> 0.01) more than third-, fourth-, and fifth-year students. On the second statement, "When a student fails in school, the teacher must accept responsibility for his failure," more than 74 percent of the sample agreed, with males significantly (> 0.02) more in agreement than females.[2] On the third statement, "All a teacher can do is present the material; it is up to the student to learn" 85 percent of the sample disagreed. Finally, 73 percent of the sample agreed that "The classroom performance of a student should be evaluated in relation to his capacities."

From the foregoing results it can be concluded that teachers in training are somewhat divided in terms of their orientation toward who should decide what children learn in school. Furthermore, there is general agreement that teachers, rather than students, should be held responsible for student failure, that students should be evaluated in terms of their capacities, and that teachers must do more than "present the material" if they want students to learn. Thus, although what the children should learn is dependent upon input from several sources, the sample feels that once decided, the teacher must accept major responsiblity for both student learning and failure.

2) *Climate for learning (Questions 32, 105, 20, 17, 28, 94, 16).* The second area of concern with regard to attitudes toward learning on the part of the sample rests with the general area of climate and includes statements concerned with teacher involvement and motivation for learning.

---

[2]In the study by Gross et al. (1968) concerning primary school teachers, 90 percent of the sample expressed positive reactions to two items that reflected a teacher's obligation to help pupils with learning difficulties, while 40 percent indicated that the pupils, not the teacher, should be held responsible for their learning difficulties.

Two statements attempted to assess the sample's orientation toward involving teachers with the personal and emotional concerns of students. The first statement read as follows: "A teacher can be effective without personally involving himself with his students." Sixty-nine percent of the sample disagreed with the statement while first- and second-year students were in significantly (> 0.006) more agreement than third-, fourth-, and fifth-year students. This orientation toward teacher involvement was sustained for the next statement as 82 percent of the sample agreed that "it is a teacher's responsibility to help students with personal problems they may have."

In terms of an ideal climate for learning, several statements were supported by the sample which indicated an orientation toward an open, as opposed to a closed, classroom setting. For example, 86 percent disagreed that "schools cannot be fun since students must work in order to learn anything worthwhile," and 90 percent agreed that "secondary school teachers should try to present materials in an entertaining way." Similarly, 94 percent concurred that "teachers should act so as to reduce the excessively competitive nature of the school system and to promote a spirit of cooperation and group effort." Additionally, when presented with the statement "student freedoms should be limited in the interest of learning," 56 percent disagreed, with females in significantly (> 0.03) more agreement than males.

Such an ideal setting, however, would apparently not find student freedoms unlimited. As noted earlier in this chapter (Section A) the sample was agreed that schools should emphasize student freedom, initiative, and creativity and that teachers should encourage students to pursue their own individual interests. At the same time there was some disagreement (54 percent) reported earlier which tends to be supported below, that students be permitted to establish their own individualized course or program of study. The additional support for the idea that the sample desires to retain some authority over student activity and learning, results from the 55 percent of the sample who agreed that "without tests and grades to prod them, most students would learn little." Thus, it may be assumed that although the student sample is positively oriented toward increasing pupil involvement in the learning process, that same sample is not as united in its

TABLE 16

Significant Multivariate and Univariate Effects and Mean Scores for Year-in-School

	Multivariate F 1.8371	df 53/450	P beyond 0.001			

Univariate F Tests (df 1/502)

Questionnaire Number	Statement	Mean Square	Univariate F	P Value	Mean Scores 1st and 2nd Year Students	Mean Scores 3rd, 4th and 5th Year Students
15	Schools should emphasize student freedom, initiative, and creativity.	2.0472	4.6523	0.03	3.549	3.727
22	Schools should emphasize the development of the intellect rather than the development of occupational skills.	10.8289	13.1062	0.0004	2.470	2.134
24	Students are influenced more by what they learn outside of school than what they learn in school.	6.4933	9.1607	0.0026	2.350	2.668
29	A strong central government is the best way to avoid inefficiency in Venezuela's educational system.	12.7944	11.5573	0.0008	2.678	2.312
31	When a student fails in school, only he is to blame.	3.8099	5.5415	0.01	1.817	1.704
32	A teacher can be effective without personally involving himself with his students.	5.5913	7.5987	0.006	2.290	2.067
36	A secondary school education is a privilege rather than a right.	3.3993	4.1684	0.04	1.899	1.704
90	Although many students are clamoring for new freedoms, few are capable of using those freedoms responsibly.	4.5822	5.8249	0.01	2.849	2.992
93	Secondary school students should be allowed to earn school credit by working in a factory or as an apprentice learning a skill.	5.8363	7.4961	0.006	2.931	3.158
97	Schools should be guided more by the individual interests of students than by the welfare of the society at large.	3.3768	5.5232	0.01	2.019	1.826
108	Pupils should participate in establishing the policies of a secondary school.	4.6696	5.0048	0.02	2.325	2.613

TABLE 17

Significant Multivariate and Univariate Effects and Mean Scores for Major

Multivariate F 1.5215   df 106/900   P beyond 0.001

Univariate F Tests (df 2/502)

Questionnaire Number	Statement	Mean Square	Univariate F	P Value	Mean Scores Pedagogy and Counseling-Administration-Evaluation	Mean Scores Humanities and Languages	Mean Scores Other Majors
18	Schools should permit students to establish their own individualized program of study rather than provide an established curriculum.	9.8953	11.0322	0.0001	2.770	2.358	2.332
21	Secondary school teachers should invite students to criticize their ideas.	3.2412	4.3567	0.01	3.416	3.200	3.152
23	Secondary school teachers should relate the content of their courses to current social problems.	1.8997	3.2802	0.03	3.540	3.479	3.352
24	Students are influenced *more* by what they learn outside of school than by what they learn in school.	3.1437	4.4352	0.01	2.677	2.503	2.361
26	It is more important for schools to develop the intellect of students than to contribute to their personal identity.	2.8451	4.3045	0.01	1.745	2.042	1.992
27	Controversial issues should be discussed in the classroom.	5.2399	6.3669	0.001	3.161	3.115	2.881
30	The student learns discipline for adult life by listening to adults.	2.5547	3.7349	0.02	2.093	2.315	2.344
90	Although many students are clamoring for new freedoms few are capable of using these freedoms responsibly.	2.7682	3.5189	0.03	2.863	3.018	2.873
103	Secondary school teachers should invite students to help make class plans or policy.	5.5290	8.0264	0.0004	3.143	2.891	2.770

TABLE 18

Significant Multivariate and Univariate Effects and Mean Scores for Sex

Multivariate F	df	P beyond
1.7208	53/450	0.002

Univariate F Tests (1/502)

Questionnaire Number	Statement	Mean Square	Univariate F	P Value	Mean Scores Males	Mean Scores Females
15	Schools should emphasize student freedom, initiative, and creativity.	2.8434	6.4616	0.01	3.730	3.558
19	Religion should be taught in school.	19.3959	22.5014	0.0001	2.004	2.386
21	Secondary school teachers should invite students to criticize their ideas.	6.9410	9.3299	0.002	3.378	3.145
24	Students are influenced *more* by what they learn outside of school than by what they learn in school.	4.1480	5.8520	0.01	2.622	2.401
27	Controversial issues should be discussed in the classroom.	5.9386	7.2158	0.007	3.133	2.955
29	A strong central government is the best way to avoid inefficiency in Venezuela's educational system.	5.5762	5.0370	0.02	2.361	2.623
34	In general, the overall curriculum taught in secondary school is relevant and useful to national development in Venezuela.	4.5638	8.3006	0.004	1.781	1.914
86	Secondary schools are designed to serve the students from middle and upper class families rather than from lower class families.	6.8142	8.6272	0.003	2.219	1.944
89	Social values are relative to a given time and place and must be continually questioned.	7.8467	7.7624	0.005	2.901	2.632
91	School is equal to life and real life problems must be emphasized in school.	3.3091	4.0553	0.04	2.914	2.709
94	Student freedoms should be limited in the interest of learning.	3.8905	4.7119	0.03	2.425	2.582
95	Schools should be concerned with providing individuals with the knowledge to solve social problems rather than with training them for specific jobs.	4.2260	4.7024	0.03	2.773	2.593
112	When a student fails in school, the teacher must accept responsibility for his failure.	4.5388	5.2536	0.02	2.991	2.751

feeling that either pupil-directed instruction or complete freedom for pupils is in the best interest of learning.

Summary and conclusions. The response to the statements in this section tends to support the idea that teachers should share the responsibility for educational decision making with parents, students, and ministerial officials. The results also suggest, however, that the sample feels that teachers rather than students should accept the responsibility for student failure and learning and should become involved with the personal and emotional concerns of students. This somewhat ideal role for the teacher, delimited by the respondents, was carried over into the area of learning climate. While disagreeing that learning cannot be fun and agreeing that teachers should present material in an entertaining way, the sample also indicated that they felt teachers should reduce the competitive nature of the classroom. A somewhat smaller percentage of the sample disagreed that student freedoms had to be limited in the interest of learning and agreed that without tests and grades to prod them, most students would learn little.

Generally, one may conclude that the student sample is anxious to serve the needs and interests of children and to see that children are able to participate in the schooling process. At the same time, it also appears that the sample is willing to take the responsiblity for student learning and failure but wishes to limit somewhat student autonomy in the learning process through retaining grades as rather traditional means of motivation and limiting student freedoms in the interest of learning.

Females along with the first- and second-year students, tended to differ from their respective counterparts in agreeing significantly more with the statement that "a teacher can be effective without personally involving himself with his students." More females than males agreed with the statement "student freedoms should be limited in the interest of learning" while more first- and second-year students than third-, fourth-, and fifth-year students agreed with the statement that "when a student fails in school, only he is to blame." Males, on the other hand, perceived the statement "when a student fails in school, the teacher must accept responsibility for his failure" more positively than females. These subgroup differences tend to reinforce the pattern mentioned earlier in this chapter, which finds that females and lower classmen are somewhat more conservative and traditional in their orientations.

Chapter Six
Occupational Selection, Prestige,
and Values

A. Occupational Selection (Appendix P)

In an expanding economy, the task of developing skilled manpower and of efficiently assigning individuals to positions within the labor market is usually assigned to the system of formal schooling. Also, schools themselves are a large employer of trained manpower and must prepare individuals for careers in education. Often, however, when it comes to competing with private and public service sectors for qualified graduates, education is usually unable to attract the most capable candidates. Furthermore, it is common for schools, especially in developing areas, to operate with large numbers of unqualified staff because they are unable to train a sufficient number of workers at the level of qualification required.

Because schools are charged with the responsibility of guiding occupational choice and certifying qualification, the role of the teacher in influencing individual student occupational decisions becomes a topic of central interest in this study. While it is apparent that out-of-school variables (i.e., parents' expectations, family status, peer group) have more influence on student academic achievement than the formal schooling process (Coleman, 1966; Central Advisory Council on Education, 1966; Averch, et al., 1972), there is no evidence to show how student occupational decision making occurs in relation to one's academic career selection. If one assumes that teachers have an impact both on guiding the educational choices of students and on socializing students into the educational-school culture, it may also be assumed that they influence the process of occupational socialization that must occur in order for a student to become a professional educator.

One section of this study was designed to examine the influence of school-related factors upon the decision of these students to become professional educators. This student population, being enrolled in a professional university program, has already made a number of definitive academic career preparation choices. Consequently, it is of specific interest to know what influences affected their personal decision to prepare as a career educator. A series of questions were asked to determine (1) why persons become teachers; (2) what factors influenced their personal decision to become teachers, and their relative importance; (3) which people most influenced this decision; (4) if, and in what way, teachers influence students' career choices; and (5) how satisfied students were with their career decision.

These questions arose, in part as a result of earlier work carried out by the Latin American Center and the Graduate School of Education at the University of California, Los Angeles, concerning the development of technical/vocational community colleges in Venezuela. It was felt that community colleges would experience difficulty in attracting secondary school graduates since, as Williams (1969) has shown in Guatemala, and Ruscoe (1968) in Venezuela, the recruitment of secondary school students depends upon competing alternative career opportunities for the relatively small number of individuals who are secondary school graduates. Furthermore, the career orientations of students have been shown to relate to socioeconomic background factors that tend to limit the population of secondary students who would most likely pursue technical/vocational careers.

Williams (1969) found that although students were trained for specific careers at the secondary level they had little intention of pursuing those careers given the material and nonmaterial rewards in alternative career patterns. Ruscoe (1968) in a study of secondary students in Venezuela concluded that national development planning was contingent upon providing long-term incentives to secondary school students. He suggested that information should be directed at lower socioeconomic students who are more likely to feel that income, working conditions, job satisfaction, and the needs of the country were important considerations when choosing an occupation. Havighurst and Gouveia (1969) complement these findings as they indicate that Brazilian secondary school student attitudes in the urban, industrial areas are more conducive to the issues related to social change. One implication of these studies is the actual and potential role of secondary school teachers in shaping student career choices. In addition, it would seem to be of some importance to discern the attitudes of potential secondary school teachers in terms of their own career decisions. An attempt was made to secure information concerning questions related to occupational and career choice and the influence that might potentially be used by teachers in orienting students into particular career patterns.

1) *Why persons become teachers (Questions 4, 6, 113, 114).* A series of questions was asked to solicit the general opinion of these students concerning why persons choose to become teachers. The first was framed in an abstract "third person" context seeking opinions concerning the general case: it asked, "why do persons usually become teachers?" The open-ended question was designed to elicit from students free responses that were not constrained by prespecified alternatives. For reporting purposes artificial categories were derived from a sampling of actual protocols and all results were categorized according to content. These results were quantifiable only in most general terms owing to the abstractness of many responses.

The responses were organized into two general groups: the first category of incentives centered primarily on individual attributes, the second was "other" oriented. About 60 percent of the sample provided the following types of reasons for why persons choose a career in teaching: vocational aptitude toward teaching, ability to teach, attitudes toward teaching, ability to understand and comprehend others, and personal satisfaction derived from teaching. The second type of response included 40 percent of the sample and concerned the contribution teachers can make to society, service to youth, contributions they can make to the profession of education, the need for teachers in the country, and the desire to educate or teach others.[1] The results suggest that the majority of students believe the principal incentives to becoming a teacher are personal orientations and individual needs for deriving satisfaction from being a teacher. They included not only

[1]Gross et al. (1968) in their study of primary school teachers in Ciudad Guayana found that 41 percent indicated their prime motive for becoming teachers was "teaching was their vocation," while 17 percent indicated it was due to a "desire to be of service to others." The study of primary teachers by Albornoz (1965), also reported a high percentage (53 percent) of the sample who indicated vocation as the primary motive.

abilities and attitudes but the desire on the part of such individuals to secure a level of satisfaction from teaching itself.

In an attempt to determine more specifically what factors influence an individual to pursue a teaching career, a companion set of questions was asked. Each of these questions was structured with alternative-response possibilities and each became more realistic by asking the respondent what factors influenced his own career choice. The first of these questions asked what "factors influenced your decision to become a secondary school teacher?" Three responses were requested. The results are summarized in table 19. It is notable that the ranking of the determining factors across choices remained constant as second and third preferences were made and total frequencies tallied (i.e., first column in table 19). The overwhelming influence motivating these students to become teachers was humanitarian — the "opportunity to help

TABLE 19

Factors that Influenced the Decision to Become a Secondary School Teacher

Determining Factor	Cumulative Number of Responses,[a] Three Choices	Percentage Responding as First Choice
1. Opportunity to help others	517	58
2. Become a professional	286	11
3. Working in a satisfying environment	222	11
4. Being creative	210	5
5. Being treated with dignity and respect	138	5
6. Job Security	109	3
7. Being in control of what you do	87	3
8. Income and financial benefits	84	2
9. Other	54	3

[a]There were 26 nonrespondents to this question but 115 of the respondents failed to provide all three requested responses.

others." The prominence of this motive seems to reverse somewhat the findings of the preceding question which observed that people become teachers more often for "service" reasons that for individual satisfactions. It is possible that the true meaning of these factors is not clearly articulated by such a dichotomization.

The second comparison question was structured to solicit the rank in importance of nine factors of the potential influence of each on the student's own career choice. The question asked each student to mark whether he thought the factors listed were "very important," "somewhat important," or "of no importance" in the selection of his career, and it also asked which of the nine factors mentioned the respondent considered the most important. The results are reported in table 20.

In contrast with the preceding question, students overwhelmingly specified the "need of the country for educators" as the most important incentive and the "opportunity to know oneself better" as the next most important. The "satisfaction derived from teaching" which was so predominant in response to the question "why do persons usually become teachers" now takes the form of "opportunity to know oneself better." Since a factor relating specifically to the teaching act was not included in the last structured question, it is not possible to relate this set of responses to the open-ended question asked earlier. Another factor that received a relatively high percentage of support from the student sample in the structured response question above was "conditions of work."

The precise forces that cause these factors to be significant are not clearly understood. For example, it is possible that the need for specialists, so clearly important, represents an awareness of pragmatic reality, the incentive offered by job opportunity. The extent to which students will enter occupations where there is high demand may indicate an ecomonic deterministic influence in their decision making. On the other hand, it is also possible that this category represents a degree of social awareness whereby students are cognizant of basic educational and societal needs and they are responding in a humanitarian way.

It is also informative to note that the majority of students found family influence, the influence of friends, the influence of "people that you have known who do the same kind of work," and the influence of teachers to be relatively "of no importance"

105

TABLE 20

Importance of Factors that Influence Career Choice

Determining Factor[a]	(In Percentages)			
	Most Important	Very Important	Somewhat Important	Of No Importance
A. Family influence, counseling or tradition	6	10	30	60
B. Conditions of work	13	26	57	18
C. Possibility of obtaining high wages	1	6	47	47
D. Opportunity to know one-self better	18	49	39	12
E. Need of the country for specialists in this career	46	74	21	5
F. Influence of teachers that you have known	6	18	35	47
G. Social prestige of the career	4	18	47	34
H. An example of the influence of people that you have known who do the same kind of work	5	18	30	51
I. Counsel or influence of friends	3	9	28	64

[a]There were 142 nonrespondents to the question.

in influencing their career selection. On the basis of this information one may conclude that individuals, irrespective of their relationship to students, are not perceived by current education majors as providing important or consequential input for career selection. Factors of "social prestige" and "high wages," too, were only moderately important in the influence they reportedly have on an individual's choosing a career in secondary education.

2) *The influence of other persons on the decision to be a teacher (Question 5).* In this same set of questions students were requested

to indicate persons who had had a major influence on their decision to become a teacher. The question asked, "which two people would you say influenced you the most in your decision to be a teacher?" When one sums the responses to both the first and second choices in this free-response question it is noted that students listed secondary school teachers as being most influential nearly twice as frequently as any other category or individual. In descending order of importance, the other responses included "friends," "self," "family," "mother," "no other person," "primary teachers," and "father."

Since the preceding structured question revealed that students, when not forced to name an individual, diminish the influence of others on their career choice, it is questionable how to weigh the importance of the last question. Considering these results as a measure of the relative influence of persons on these decisions, it is striking that secondary teachers head the list by a relatively wide margin over the next most important individuals. It suggests not only that there is a great potential for the secondary teacher to influence individual student decision making, and that teachers are apparently affecting students' lives, but also that education students believe that secondary teachers have the potential to influence their students.

3) *The influence of teachers on career choice (Questions 13, 14).* A further elucidation of this point was obtained in yet another question which asked whether or not teachers do, in fact, "influence their students' career choices. Sixty-three percent of the student sample indicated that they thought teachers did have an influence on their students' selection of a career, providing further evidence to support the supposition that important persons influence career choice. In an attempt to understand how this influence might occur, an inquiry was made of those who responded affirmatively that "teachers had an influence on student career selection." It was a free-response question asking *how* teachers influence their students' career choices. The largest number of respondents reported that teachers influenced student choices by providing vocational orientation and by directing students toward areas of interest or ability. The second most frequent response related to influencing student choices by the manner in which teachers present material. The third manner of

107

influence pertained to the communication of facts and information regarding job opportunities and requirements. Other categories included preferential treatment of students, providing role examples, and communicating personal opinions.

This set of responses suggest that there is a tendency for education students to perceive the influence of the teacher in both a deliberate and nondeliberate way. In the deliberate mode, teachers are able to influence student career choice by directing them to areas of student interest and ability or by providing vocational information. Since school counselors are few in Venezuela, the counseling of students is often assumed as a matter of course by teachers. On the other hand, some education students tend to feel that teachers influence student career choice in a more nondeliberate fashion by providing a role model, by communicating opinions, by reacting to students in a certain way and by influencing student choices by means of biased curricular presentations. This issue lies at the very heart of the assumption that schools and teachers may influence student decision making and career aspirations and therefore demands much more research and observation.

B. Occupational Prestige (Appendix Q)

Status differentials between occupations are known to have some influence upon professional stratification. Hoyle (1969) has argued, for example, that within the sector of education alone status differentials create artificial prestige differences between levels of position which cause teachers to seek promotion to administrative or directorate positions of higher status. Hoyle attributes this desire for a gain in status to a feeling of relative social deprivation which results from social stratification. In acknowledging the conflict that arises between one's own professional commitment and his perception of career success, he suggests that teachers often reflect a good deal of ambiguity in their opinions regarding the prestige of their profession.

Bernbaum (1969) has verified that prospective entrants to the teaching profession are, indeed, sensitive to different prestige categories within the teaching profession and the educational system. He shows, however, that there is a trend toward narrowing these differentials. While it is unclear how prestige and status perceptions influence students' career aspirations, it does seem that prestige is differentially associated with occupational categories and that rankings of occupational prestige are fairly constant both over time and cross-nationally (Bendix and Lipset, 1966).

Sociologists have frequently shown the importance of status to adolescents. Whether or not this influence evolves in Latin American cultures in the same way as it does in the United States is a question for social research. There is evidence, however, that the concept of status and prestige is highly influential within elite-ordered societies, and numerous social scientists would describe the general Latin American culture as dominated by various elitist groups.

The growing body of literature, along with the importance of describing occupational status and prestige as perceived by prospective teachers who themselves have the potential of influencing student career choice, prompted us to include in this work a measure of occupational prestige, including various professional education categories.

1) *Prestige ranking (Questions 10, 11)*. Since no information was uncovered concerning either occupational classifications in Venezuela or the perceptions of education students regarding such classifications, a list of thirty-two occupations, each with a five-point scale rating from low to high, was included in the questionnaire. The set of questions was designed to, first, elicit conceptions of the prestige of a series of occupations, second, rank the most prestigeful, and third, identify the three most important for Venezuela's current needs. Since prospective secondary school teachers have been shown to perceive their roles as being important in shaping career decisions, the information gleaned from the questionnaire should assist those concerned with directing toward identified national needs not only teachers but also future secondary student generations.

The first question in the series asked individuals to rate each of the thirty-two occupations on a five-point scale from "very low" to "very high" (table 21). The student ranking of occupations by prestige reflected the placement of a high priority on educational positions: the position of primary school teacher was ranked twelfth from the highest in prestige, director of a secondary

TABLE 21

Occupational Prestige Rankings

Occupation[a]	Mean	Standard Deviation
Investigador Científico	4.520	0.811
Profesor universitario	4.364	0.730
Médico	4.282	0.685
Ingeniero	4.159	0.688
Profesor secundaria	3.959	0.833
Economista	3.859	0.674
Director de escuela secundaria	3.834	0.811
Alto empleado gubernamental	3.801	1.092
Oficial de Fuerzas Armadas	3.640	1.059
Abogado	3.520	0.883
Técnico de laboratorio	3.506	0.828
Periodista	3.482	0.754
Maestro escuela primaria	3.454	1.062
Hombre de negocios	3.361	0.887
Hacendado	3.340	0.956
Trabajador social	3.337	0.818
Sacerdote	3.216	1.090
Músico	3.125	0.894
Contador	3.075	0.707
Actor	3.027	0.949
Enfermero	2.988	0.975
Electricista	2.897	0.797
Jugador de béisbol	2.843	0.835
Monja	2.773	1.079
Oficinista	2.731	0.708
Secretaria	2.644	0.685
Trabajador agrícola	2.621	1.112
Capataz en una fábrica	2.445	0.779
Caporal en una hacienda	2.384	0.888
Soldado	2.198	1.041
Policía	2.058	1.047
Limpiador de calle	1.859	1.060

[a]See Appendix Q for English translation.

school was ranked seventh, secondary school teacher fifth, and university professor second.

When the students were asked to rank the five most prestigious occupations, the total number of responses across the five choices indicated that scientific investigator, university professor, medical doctor, secondary school teacher, and engineer, in that order, constituted the hierarchy. Once again, the status accorded scientific investigator, university professor, and secondary teacher, are worthy of note.

2) *Venezuela's occupational needs (Question 12).* When asked to list the three occupations most important for national development in Venezuela, the sample responded with the following occupations in their order of cumulative preference: engineer, scientific investigator, medical doctor, economist, and secondary school teacher. It is important to note that although it was a free-response question, the occupational-needs hierarchy tends to resemble closely the prestige hierarchy mentioned above and once again demonstrates the perception of students regarding the need for secondary school teachers.

A set of artificial occupational categories was created to identify which sector of the work force demanded the most urgent attention according to students. In the order of most frequent mention, the categories were technology (engineer, scientific investigator, laboratory technician, etc.); teaching (primary, secondary, and university); professional (medical doctor, lawyer, etc.); followed by agriculture, and, finally, industry. One may suggest that the overwhelming concern for national development among this group was focused on the general area of technological growth and the area of professional education and teaching.

3) *Alternative career choice (Question 62).* The final question in this series asked the student to analyze his career choice in terms of possible alternatives. If he was given the opportunity to start over again, and he had sufficient means, for what kind of work would he prepare himself? Half the sample would pursue an academic career; 21 percent would pursue a professional career; 18 percent had not thought sufficiently to answer the question; and approximately 9 percent indicated business, technical or craft work, and the arts. In other words, about 30 percent would change their careers while 50 percent would most likely repeat a similar course of study. There was a slight trend among fourth-year students, when compared with first-year students, to indicate a stronger likelihood of altering their career choice if given the opportunity to begin again.

111

When comparing the response to this question with the data presented in Chapter Three that 85 percent of the sample thought they would be teaching five years hence, there is apparently 30 percent of the sample who is currently entering the teaching profession with some conscious dissatisfaction. One might pursue the question in order to better comprehend reasons for leaving the teaching career after only a relatively short experience. For example, do the students who would alter their career patterns if given the opportunity end up being the most likely to leave the profession after a short period of time in the classroom and is it possible to identify such individuals while they are still enrolled in the university?

C. Work Values (See Appendix R, Questions 73-80)

The attitudes or predispositions of individuals are assumed to relate to a wide variety of both individual and social consequences. Psychological determinists often attribute societal advancement and superiority to causal forces deriving from individual "need-achievement" or status recognition seeking. Indeed, whether we can credit such psychodynamic characteristics with the success of the landed aristocracy of England, or the entrepreneurs of Antioquia in Colombia, is speculative, but it is safe to assume that there exists a strong relationship between the values of people and the level of socioeconomic development.

It is not whether modern attitudes and values are prede-terminants of development that is important to this study, but rather it is the importance of such predispositions in terms of influencing individual decision making. Individuals make choices that determine their academic pursuits and their eventual occupation. It is one of the assumptions of this inquiry that the distribution of individuals within the economy and society has a strong influence on social development, and that the educational and occupational decisions made by individuals in a democratic society are very important in reflecting both the incentives of the market place and the priorities of individuals. [2]

---

[2]While the dynamics that relate educational pursuits to occupational aspiration and later to job success are not known, it is clear that there is an association between education and occupational stratification (Collins, 1971), and that the selection of academic careers does not occur entirely within a "free market" environment.

One of the factors that apparently influences career aspirations is a measure of ambition or "risk-taking." Psychometric measures indicate that individuals are distributed along a continuum with regard to personal ambition and that they are willing to act upon these inherent desires to the extent that they will take risks in an attempt to achieve success.

Because individual predisposing factors are suspected to influence educational and occupational choice, a measure of personal ambition and risk-taking was included in the questionnaire. The instrument used was developed by Lawrence K. Williams (1962) and has been used by William F. Whyte in Peru (1962) and by Robert J. Havighurst and A. J. Gouveia in Brazil (1969). One reason for the selection of this scale was that it had been used on Latin American populations and, therefore, provided some comparative data.

Williams Risk-Taking Scale. Williams developed his scale as a measure of the propensity to take risks versus the propensity to seek security. He devised eight pairs of briefly stated job characteristics which were given in a forced-choice form to respondents who were asked to select one of each pair as their preference. As the items are drawn from a single universe[3] the score for this scale is a simple count of the number of responses made preferring the job described as "the student's desire for autonomy or self-direction in his work and willingness to take risks" (Havighurst, 1969: 137). The score may range from 0 to 8, and the mean is usually about 4.[4] The risk-taking instrument used in the present study is presented below.

[3]Guttman scale analysis was used to derive Williams's original instrument. Havighurst and Gouveia in Brazil and Whyte in Peru found, however, through using factor analytic techniques that there were seemingly not one but three factors to this scale. The Peruvian and Brazilian investigations, however, disagreed as to what these factors were. Whyte noted that attitude toward work autonomy, attitude toward risk-taking for the sake of success, and attitude toward work which offers challenge as one of its rewards were the three factors, while Havighurst and Gouveia found autonomy (items 1, 2, 5), risk-taking (items 4, 6, 7, 8) and preference for general rather than specific instructions (item 3), as the three factors.

[4]In determining means of the sample, a score of one for each risk-taking response was given. If an individual failed to respond to two or more of the items, his profile was omitted from final tabulation. If an individual failed to respond to one item, he was given his modal score from the other items. Out of the 636 students who responded to this set of questions, only 30 failed to indicate their preference on two or more of the eight items.

1. I prefer: (check one)
    a. A job where I am almost always on my own.
    b. A job where there is nearly always someone available to help me on problems that I don't know how to handle.

2. I prefer: (check one)
    a. A job where I have to make many decisions by myself.
    b. A job where I have to make a few decisions by myself.

3. I prefer: (check one)
    a. A job where my instructions are quite detailed and specific.
    b. A job where my instructions are very general.

4. I prefer: (check one)
    a. A job where I am almost always certain of my ability to perform well.
    b. A job where I am usually pressed to the limit of my abilities.

5. I prefer: (check one)
    a. A job where I am the final authority on my work.
    b. A job where there is nearly always a person or a procedure that will catch my mistakes.

6. I prefer: (check one)
    a. A job where I could be either highly successful or a complete failure.
    b. A job where I could never be too successful but neither could I be a complete failure.

7. I prefer: (check one)
    a. A job that is changing very little.
    b. A job that is constantly changing.

8. I prefer: (check one)
    a. An exciting job but one which might be done away within a short time.
    b. A less exciting job but one which would undoubtedly exist in the company for a long time.

Table 22 presents the results of the risk-taking scale among the Venezuelan sample as well as that of the three previous studies conducted in the United States, Brazil, and Peru,[5] and it permits a comparison among the several groups on both the percentage choosing the risk-taking option as well as on overall mean scores.

Item 1, where the person chooses between a job in which he is on his own or in which there is someone on hand to help him with

[5]The results of the three previous studies shown in table 22 are taken from Havighurst and Gouveia (1969:273).

114

TABLE 22

Comparison of U.S.A., Peru, Brazil, and Venezuela on Job Preference
Inventory of Risk-Taking Scale

(Percentage favoring a given characteristic of job)

Item Number	Characteristic	USA Adults	Peru Adults		Peru Boys		Brazil Boys		Venezuela	
		White Collar	Middle Class	Working Class	Public School	Private School	North Brazil	South Brazil	Men	Women
1	Own directions	77	59	41	60	69	71	82	69	73
2	Many decisions	80	87	77	62	63	66	81	84	82
3	General Instructions	52	49	26	24	28	40	35	18	16
4	Ability Pressed	25	39	33	40	39	29	46	7	4
5	Final authority	66	91	86	39	69	67	74	52	59
6	Success or failure	45	75	70	65	78	30	54	78	81
7	Constant change	61	68	42	22	30	61	79	66	66
8	Exciting job	17	44	39	25	44	30	55	46	42
	Mean score	4.18	5.12	4.14	3.37	4.20	3.92	5.06	4.18	4.15

115

problems, finds the Venezuelan students preferring to be on their own. The students compare favorably with Peruvian boys and adults but are less likely to prefer autonomy than are United States adults or Brazilian secondary school boys.

With regard to item 2, the Venezuelan sample indicated their general preference for a job where they have to make many decisions by themselves. Only the Peruvian middle class adults exceed the percentage of Venezuelan students choosing this option.

The results of item 3 suggest that the Venezuelan sample prefers detailed and specific rather than general instructions in their jobs, contrary to what might have been anticipated given the data of the comparison populations. This finding may be due, in part, to the nature of the teaching profession itself. Prospective teachers have been instructed throughout their careers on such pedagogical practices as lesson planning and preparing units of instruction. In addition, as university students, they have been directed as to what to study and how to prepare assignments. In other words, in terms of both their ideal professional role model as well as in their customary activities as students they have come to expect and support rather specific and detailed instructions. It may be assumed that the sample would find general and diffuse instructions unproductive for their chosen careers.

Item 4, too, offers results opposite from what might have been anticipated given the findings of the other studies. The Venezuelan sample chose overwhelmingly the response that indicated preference for a job where they would amost always be certain of their ability to perform well rather than the response where they would have a job that would press them to the limit of their abilities. Once again, the most plausible reason for the preference would seem to rest with the nature of the teaching profession itself. The results presented earlier in this chapter suggest that one of the prime reasons individuals become teachers is the existence of a vocational aptitude toward teaching. In other words, students become aware of teacher role requirements and they assume that, because of their own particular aptitudes, they can become successful teachers. The perception, then, is not one that demands that a person be pushed to the limit of his abilities but instead one that takes advantage of the

116

abilities (vocational aptitude) that already exist.[6] The result is complete compatibility between the expectations of the professional role and the inherent abilities of the individual aspiring to that role.

The fifth item finds the Venezuelan students somewhat less inclined than the other groups studied to prefer having final authority over their work. This may relate once again to their extended experiences as students where they have become accustomed to others, primarily teachers, checking and correcting their work. In their future positions as teachers they are likely to find somewhat greater autonomy than they did as students although they will likely face a new group of masters including the school principal and the parents in the community where they teach.

Items 6, 7, and 8 find the Venezuelan sample comparing favorably with the other studies using the risk-taking scale. In item 6, they prefer a job where either complete success or failure can be achieved; in item 7 the sample preferred a job that undergoes constant change; in item 8 they tend to favor somewhat a job that is less exciting but which will likely be in existence for a relatively long period of time rather than a job that is exciting but which might be done away with in a short time.[7]

Factors such as those included in the risk-taking scale provide only a few components of a total constellation of elements which in interaction combine to explain an individual's career choice. The fact that a similar percentage of males and females indicated similar preferences tends to support the apparent influence that the education profession has on its prospective members. Whether such congruence can be attributed to anticipatory socialization, to the professional curriculum, or to a prior self-selecting mechanism remains to be tested. Although males and females have been

[6] An emerging belief among some scholars of occupational decision making is that students select careers not where they will maximize their status/income but where they can maximize the probability of their *success* in an acceptable status/income position (Martin Carnoy, personal communication).

[7] It is important to note that cross-cultural comparisons are subject to problems of validity since little control can be exercised over either the translation or the administration of the instrument. The use of overall scale scores rather than single items for comparisons across national and cultural boundaries are perhaps more likely to give valid results.

shown to differ significantly with regard to certain attitudinal items reported earlier in this study, it is apparent that in terms of risk-taking they perceive their job preferences similarly and represent a rather homogeneous population. This is especially apparent with items 3 and 4 where the two groups are similar but differ considerably from the other adult and youth populations investigated in Latin America and the United States.

Chapter Seven
Summary of Findings

This investigation was designed to survey the attitudes and values of Venezuelan prospective secondary school personnel in terms of professional expectations and orientations, national development priorities, educational goals, and occupational selection and prestige. It is assumed that such personnel are important to national and local educational plans and development priorities. Because the financial support of school personnel in Venezuela, as elsewhere, accounts for the major portion of the educational budget, and because the faith placed in formal schools for stability and change in society inevitably rests with such personnel, the analysis of their attitudes and values is thought to be essential for educational planning and reform.

A. The Sample

The sample of 638 students was drawn from four universities and the two pedogogic institutes representing different geographic regions in Venezuela. Prospective secondary school teachers, counselors, administrators, and measurement specialists were included in the sample.

Approximately 72 percent of the sample were enrolled in the pedagogic institutes at Barquisimeto and Caracas and represented the majority of the students intending to become teachers. The remainder of the sample was drawn from the University of Los Andes, the University of Oriente, Central University, and Andrés Bello University and constituted the majority of the students pursuing careers as secondary school counselors, administrators, and measurement specialists as well as those majoring in pedagogy.

In terms of background factors, 74 percent of the sample had parents who had completed primary school or less; 12 percent of the parents were foreign born; 15 percent of the students reported that their mothers worked outside of the home; 50 percent of the students lived with their parents while enrolled in school.

The sample included 59 percent females and 41 percent males. The females were younger than males and reported having parents who had achieved a higher level of education. The average age of the sample was twenty-five, with the majority between twenty-two and twenty-eight. Students whose parents completed secondary education or higher were all below age twenty-six.

Approximately 75 percent of the sample was single, and of this group, a higher proportion were females. Eighty-six percent of the sample reported growing up in a city or town of more than 2,000 inhabitants. Males and older students predominated among the 43 percent who reported working while enrolled in their respective institutions. Of those who worked, 50 percent did so for twenty hours or less per week, and 80 percent were teaching at the primary or secondary level.

Eighty-one percent of the students attended federal or state public secondary schools while 14 percent attended private Catholic schools. Fifty-seven percent had graduated from secondary school since 1966. Academic secondary institutions were attended by 75 percent of the sample, while normal schools were attended by 19 percent. Of those who attended academic secondary institutions, 46 percent majored in the sciences and 28 percent in the humanities. Forty percent of the sample graduated from secondary schools with twenty-six to fifty classmates, while 50 percent graduated with a class of more than fifty students.

A positive relationship was found between major at secondary school and major at the university. Commercial and technical secondary school majors as well as academic science majors were likely to enroll in similar majors at the university level. Humanities majors were equally distributed across pedagogy, counseling-evaluation-administration, humanities, and languages at the university level whereas normal school graduates were likely to enroll in these majors with the exception of languages.

Physical science, natural science, humanities, counseling-evaluation-administration, and pedagogy majors accounted for approximately 16 percent of the sample, respectively, while language majors constituted 12 percent, and commercial and nonclassifiable, physical education, and technical-vocational education accounted for less than 4 percent each. Twenty-four percent of the sample was enrolled in their first year, 32 percent in their second year, 15 percent in their third year, 28 percent in their fourth year, and 1 percent in their fifth year of studies. Thirty-two percent reported that they had practice-teaching experience.

Eighty percent of the sample claimed Catholicism as their religion, with males more likely not to claim any religion. Politically, one-third of the sample reported being moderate, 17 percent on the left, and 4 percent on the right. About 33 percent indicated that they preferred not to indicate their political orientations. Some may find the moderate and left orientation to be low, although one hypothesize that professional educators are generally more moderate and sometimes conservative in their political orientations. The relatively high percentage of students preferring not to respond to the question may result from general anxiety and mistrust of this type of survey and its effect on later job placement, or from the political climate existing in Venezuela at the time of the survey.

The evidence gathered suggests considerable intergenerational educational mobility among the majority of the sample population. The fact that 50 percent of the sample had parents who had not graduated from primary school attests to this mobility. Without knowing how such mobility compares with other professions, the data enables one to conclude that the teaching profession is an important path for mobility in Venezuela. Given the recent development of mass education facilities in Venezuela resulting from the movement toward a more democratic political climate as suggested in Chapter One, this mobility within the education profession may relate to the increased access and opportunity to pursue formal schooling evident in Venezuela during the past ten to fifteen years. The opportunity structure may also account for the increased number of women pursuing education careers when traditionally the field has been dominated by males. Since males evidenced greater mobility than females, the results indicate that males from higher status (education) backgrounds have yet to turn to education as a professional career. The latter conclusion may be changing, however, since the results suggest that younger students are from better-educated families. Thus, along with access to educational facilities, the roles of males and females with respect to occupational choice appear to be changing, as attested to by the heavier influx of women and

121

an increasing tendency among young students to be from better education backgrounds.

The sample population is not inexperienced in terms of prior teaching responsibilities; of 43 percent of the students who reported working while pursuing their university studies, 80 percent were involved in teaching activities. In addition, about 32 percent reported having had practice-teaching experience. The results suggest that although these students are being prepared in a preservice program, many are not naively approaching this field without prior contacts with students in a teaching-learning situation, a point that should be kept in mind as the results of this study are analyzed and compared with other national or subnational data. In other words, it is questionable how many students preparing for careers in education in other countries would have had such experiences prior to being credentialed.

Other conclusions drawn from this primarily demographic data are that prospective secondary school personnel are largely from urban settings and graduates of academic secondary institutions. Since Venezuela has virtually no rural secondary schools, this urban bias is expected and explains in part why most students desire to work in large urban centers upon graduation. The fact that the majority of the students graduated from academic secondary institutions is less easily explained even though universities require that an academic secondary diploma be obtained before being admitted as a regular student. Although the pedagogic institutes have no such requirement, normal school graduates do not appear to prefer these institutions over universities.

B. Professional Expectations and Orientations

Ninety-four percent of the sample intended to work in secondary schools. The majority of these individuals were planning to become full- or part-time teachers and to still be teaching within five years. In addition, those students who were majoring in subject matter areas commonly included in the secondary school curriculum were committed to teaching the same subjects for which they were being trained at their respective institutions.

Of those who reported they would not pursue a career in secondary schools, the majority were planning to remain in the professional education field by pursuing further university studies, teaching at a level other than secondary, or becoming involved in administration or educational research. The majority of those who reported that they would not be teaching in five years indicated they would be studying at a university. One may conclude that the members of the sample are highly committed to pursuing the career for which they are being trained. The results of this survey suggest if more than 6 percent of the sample leaves the positions for which they are being trained at the secondary school level, the cause will apparently not be related to their expressed intentions while undergoing that training but instead will relate to personal and social factors yet undetermined.

Ninety-four percent of the sample intended to seek positions in public federal or public state schools rather than religious-sponsored institutions. In addition, 75 percent of the students were planning to work in academic as opposed to normal or technical secondary schools. The sample's preferences and expectations for the geographical location of the secondary school where they intended to work was related positively to the location of the institute or university where they were enrolled. Two-thirds of the students anticipated working in Caracas, Barquisimeto, San Cristóbal, or another major city, with only 12 percent intending to teach in a small city or town. Thirty-one percent of the sample felt that it would be necessary to earn additional income by working at a second job once a teaching position was secured. Most of these individuals planned to acquire a second teaching position or involve themselves in business enterprises in order to earn this supplementary income.

The data concerning student perceptions of teacher's unions indicated that 98 percent found such organizations necessary and 75 percent were planning to become members. A slight majority of the students thought that unions were necessary in order to improve schools for children while the remaining students thought they were necessary to improve teaching as a profession or to improve working conditions for teachers.

The majority of the sample were not intending to become heavily involved in the administration of the school where they would teach. Instead, they indicated that they would be satisfied if they had an opportunity to express their opinions or to be consulted on matters that concerned them. When asked how an official from the Ministry of Education would react if a teacher indicated that a ministerial ruling would prove harmful to education in Venezuela, 36 percent of the students said the official would pay some attention to the teacher's opinion, while 43 percent said he would pay little attention or totally ignore the opinion. The students were also asked how likely it would be that they would attempt to influence the Ministry if the occasion arose. Fifty-four percent replied that it was very likely or somewhat likely that they would take the opportunity to influence the official. The sample then responded to a question concerning the teaching of material that contradicted a teacher's values and beliefs. The majority replied that they would teach the material even though it contradicted their orientations and that they would include either their own or alternative points of view.

Finally, data were reported concerning religious beliefs and practices as well as the teaching of religion in schools. While 80 percent of the sample indicated that they were Catholics, only 45 percent said that they occasionally, regularly, or always participated in religious activities. Half the respondents felt that religious beliefs and faith were essential or helpful to the good teacher, while the other half felt that such faith and beliefs were not important, or hindered the good teacher. Forty percent of the sample felt that religion should be taught in school while the remaining 60 percent disagreed. Responses to several of the questions concerning religion indicated a strong positive relationship between religiousness and the level of education achieved by parents through the completion of the secondary school.

C. Venezuelan Educational Needs and Development Priorities

The students felt that the three most critical needs of education in Venezuela today were: first, insufficient or ill-prepared professors and staff; second, insufficient or inadequate schools or classes; and third, a need for restructuring the educational system and its programs. The ranking of the preferences generally remained the same whether one was concerned with the first choice of the sample or the cumulative responses across the three choices.

In response to the question, "if only one thing could be changed in relation to secondary schooling, what do you think it should be," the sample indicated that their first concern was with restructuring the educational system while their second and third concerns were directed at improving the school curriculum and improving student-teacher relationships including methods of teaching.

The distinct responses to these two questions were felt to relate to the specific emphasis in the latter question toward changes in the secondary schools as opposed to the emphasis on education in the former question on critical needs in general. Thus, the members of the sample were more likely to view education in Venezuela as needing more and better schools and staff while they saw secondary schools in need of a general restructuring with special emphasis on curricular change.

When asked to choose from a list of factors that might possibly limit educational quality in Venezuela, the sample indicated that the interference of partisan politics, large class size, limited financial allocations, and a lack of teaching materials were, in that order, the most important.

On the types of schools needed most by Venezuela, the preference was for university and secondary technical institutes, supporting a functional and utilitarian orientation toward schooling. The second most needed school type, according to the sample, was the preschool, which was felt to relate to the need for child care and formal socialization in urban Venezuela as well as to the recent educational research demonstrating the importance of the early childhood years in terms of affective and cognitive development.

Two questions were posed to assess the students' attitudes toward national development priorities. The first concerned the three most critical goals of Venezuela in terms of national development. The students indicated that the government should be concerned primarily with providing greater educational opportunity and secondarily with industrial and economic development. In addition, they reported that attention should be directed toward increasing social awareness and restructuring the educational system. The companion question solicited opinions regarding what the Venezuelan government, rather than the students themselves, felt to be the important national goals. The sample perceived the government as promoting high level, trained manpower, industrial development, and increased educational opportunities.

125

The student sample was generally oriented toward change within the educational system, calling for a restructuring of programs along with a general improvement and expansion of both staff and schools. Partisan politics, class size, budgetary support, and a lack of teaching materials were felt to be factors limiting educational quality. Priorities were on technical/vocational schools and preschools, with the former relating positively to the student's concern for industrial and economic development. Generally, the sample tended to emphasize educational opportunity and expansion of national development priorities whereas they perceived the government as placing more attention on the training of high-level manpower. Both factors relate to the importance of education in the development process.

D. Attitudes Toward Education

The sample viewed occupational preparation as the primary purpose of secondary education, and meeting the needs and objectives of society in general as the primary purpose of education in general. Thus, the orientation was rather pragmatic, with intellectual values placed in a position of lesser importance. The findings suggest an openness to the current national development priorities in Venezuela and a readiness to subscribe to planning efforts. In addition, it appeared that the sample would be willing to share some of its educational responsibilities with institutions other than schools, especially institutions concerned with occupational training. An emphasis was also placed on addressing controversial issues and real-life problems through the school curriculum. Males, pedagogy-administration-evaluation majors, and students enrolled in their later years of study, rather than their respective counterparts, were inclined to be most flexible and liberal in their attitudes toward what the purposes of education should be.

The sample generally supported the idea that schools are capable of changing society by instilling attitudes and values in students but felt that the present school curriculum is not appropriate for fostering such change. Schools were thought to be more important for citizenship training than parents of the community thus demonstrating a bias in favor of planned, institutionalized programs of instruction. The sample viewed secondary school as a right rather than a privilege and felt that secondary school graduates should be prepared to engage in physical work. There was an equal division among the members of the sample as to whether upper class parents prepare their children to achieve at a higher level than lower class parents, while there was considerable disagreement that the secondary school is designed to better serve the needs of middle and upper class families than those of lower class families. The significant differences among subgroups by the various items tended to support the trend already mentioned. Males, pedagogy and counseling-administration-evaluation majors, and students enrolled in their third, fourth, and fifth year of studies were generally more critical and liberal than females, other majors, and students enrolled in their first two years of study.

Regarding the series of attitude statements directed toward school management and participation in decision-making activities, the items placed an emphasis on government, teacher, student, and parent involvement. Generally, the responses indicated an orientation toward both centralized and decentralized policies for school decision making. In this regard, the sample expressed both a need for a major role for teachers in terms of such operations and the need for a strong central government to manage the educational system. Student involvement in secondary school policy formulation was viewed less favorably than student involvement in the instructional process at the classroom level, while at the same time the sample generally concurred that although "students are clamoring for new freedoms, few are capable of using those freedoms responsibly." The sample was divided in its attitude toward parents and professional educators as to who should make final decisions about education, while at the same time the sample supported the idea that parental involvement in school and educational functions is necessary and important.

Males were more favorable toward teachers inviting students to criticize their ideas and, along with upper classmen, were less favorable toward the need for a strong central government to avoid inefficiency in Venezuela's educational system. Students in their last three years of school were in more agreement than other students that pupils should participate in the establishment of secondary school policy, and similarly, that few students are capable of using new-found freedoms responsibly. Pedagogy and counseling-administration-evaluation majors were in more

127

agreement than other majors that students should be invited to help make class plans or policy and that teachers should invite students to criticize their ideas. Humanities and language majors were in most agreement that few of the students who are seeking new freedoms are actually capable of using such freedoms responsibly.

The last section of concern in this area is the sample's perceptions regarding student learning, with special emphasis on student and teacher involvement in the learning process and on the climate under which learning occurs.

The results indicated that the sample is inclined to support sharing with parents, students, and ministerial officials the responsibility for educational decision-making, including what is taught. Teachers rather than students, however, were felt to be the ones to be held responsible for student failure and learning. In the area of learning climate, the sample disagreed that learning cannot be fun and agreed that teachers should present material in an entertaining way. Furthermore, it was felt that teachers should reduce the emphasis on competition in the classroom. There was general disagreement that student freedoms had to be limited in the interest of learning and general agreement that without tests and grades to prod them, most students would learn little. The subgroup differences in this section continued to reinforce the patterns mentioned above, that is, females and lower classmen were somewhat more conservative and traditional in their orientations than their respective counterparts.

E. Occupational Selection, Prestige, and Values

A series of questions was asked to determine (1) why persons become teachers, (2) what factors influence a personal decision to become a teacher, (3) which people are most influential in this decision, (4) if, and in what way teachers influence students' career choices, and (5) how satisfied students are with their career decision. The results suggest that people become teachers either because of a vocational aptitude and a positive predisposition toward teaching (self-satisfaction) or because of the contribution teachers are able to make to their society and to others (serving others). These two orientations were found to be dependent on whether the question asked was open-ended or whether it involved a selection among a series of structured alternatives and whether the question was directed to the individual himself or asked the individual to make judgments as to why others might choose education as a career.

When directed to indicate the relative importance of certain factors on career choice, the majority of the students indicated that "other persons" were of little or no importance. When asked, "which two people would you say influenced you the most in your decision to be a teacher?" however, the students indicated that secondary school teachers were most influential. In addition, a majority of the students felt that teachers do, in fact, influence their students' career choices either in a deliberate (e.g., providing information) or nondeliberate (e.g., acting as a role model) way.

The results suggest that prospective secondary school personnel generally perceive the teacher as a potential source of influence on student career choice. In a country that is currently experiencing shortages of technical-vocational middle-level manpower, the evidence would seem to suggest the possibility of supplying information to prospective secondary school personnel concerning current and anticipated manpower needs so that as teachers they would be better equipped to guide their students toward occupational goals that fulfill not only the students' individual aspirations but the objectives of the wider society as well.

Regarding the level of satisfaction evidenced by the sample toward their current career choice, 30 percent said that if given the opportunity to begin again they would change their careers. Such evidence raises the issue of dissatisfaction with the educational profession before entering it and suggests the possibility of identifying such individuals before they assume teaching or other educational positions in an attempt to reduce rapid turnover within the profession.

The sample was directed to indicate the prestige of a list of thirty-two occupations and to identify the three occupations most important for Venezuela's current needs. As might be anticipated, a prestige ranking of high priority was accorded to educational career positions. When the students were asked to rank the five most prestigious occupations, the hierarchy included scientific investigator, university professor, medical doctor, engineer, and secondary school teacher. In listing the occupations most important for national development in Venezuela, the sample gave the following occupations in their order of cumulative preference: engineer, scientific investigator, medical doctor, economist, and secondary school teacher. As is evident, both the prestige ranking and the needs hierarchy were similar. The areas of technological growth and professional education emerged as the most prominent concerns for national development.

A set of questions concerning risk-taking showed the mean scores of the sample to compare favorably with other United States and Latin American populations for whom results are available. Item analysis reveals that both males and females in the Venezuelan sample perceive risk-taking similarly. Generally, they prefer a job where (1) they are able to make many decisions by themselves, (2) where they are almost always on their own, (3) where they have final authority over their work, (4) where there is constant change, (5) where instructions are detailed and specific, (6) where they can be either highly successful or a complete failure, (7) where they are certain of their abilities to perform well, and (8) where the job is less exciting but will exist for a long period of time.

The item analysis also reveals distinctions that set the Venezuelan sample off from the other tested populations, most prominently the need for detailed and specific instructions and the notion that they must have a job where they are certain of their abilities to perform well. It is argued that such orientations are very likely related to the activities inherent in the professional education role model and in the sample's current status as university students.

F. Conclusions

The sample perceives formal schooling as an indispensable tool in changing society and in meeting the needs of a developing economy. There is a tendency to value secondary schools for occupational preparation rather than for intellectual or personal goals, while for education in general the objective is to relate schools to society's wider needs. One may assume that because of the considerable educational mobility manifested by this population, such faith in schools is to be expected. Since the mobility occurred during a rapid expansion of school facilities and under somewhat special circumstances, specifically the change from dictatorial to democratic politics during the fifties and sixties, it is questionable how long it can be sustained and evidenced in future professional cohorts. The positive bias toward education and the schools is also present in the sample's view of educators in Venezuelan society. When compared with other occupations, the sample places educators high in terms of prestige and high on the list of Venezuela's needs.

Other indicators of this vested interest in schools are present when the development priorities of the sample are assessed. The students feel that formal education should be the first priority of Venezuela's development goals whereas they perceive the government to be more prone to favor industrial and economic priorities. Although education and economic goals are far from incompatible, it is nevertheless striking that the students would differentiate between their own as opposed to the government's aims and that they would assume that schools are more likely to change society rather than be changed by it.

Another indication of the sample's faith in schools to change society arises from their feeling that schooling is not biased in favor of the middle and upper classes. Once again this is assumed to be partially explained by the fact that their own mobility was achieved through the schools. It is questionable how such a view can be sustained, however, when past research indicates a high positive relationship between social class and school success. The studies by J. Coleman in the United States, the Central Advisory Council on Education in England, and T. Husein in twelve developed countries all indicate that the major portion of the variance in cognitive success of students in school derives from the social class background of the students. If one accepts such evidence, the rather optimistic orientation of the students in this sample is likely the result of faith, personal experience, and a lack of knowledge of the sociological interface between schools and their clients.

While my observations are grounded in the data, it is apparent that the sample is critical of the condition of the schooling enterprise in Venezuela. The rather deep dissatisfaction with several aspects of the system is evidenced by the student's inclination to see a need for better professors and staff in schools and, more specifically regarding the secondary level, a need for restructuring the system with considerable curricular and

131

instructional alteration. One may question whether the planned comprehensive high schools in Venezuela will act to satisfy this criticism. The revised system will more likely satisfy this group of individuals if it incorporates considerable curricular and instructional rather than organizational and structural change. For example, although they were primarily academic secondary school graduates, the students seem to be rebelling against an intellectual bias in the schools. They tend to prefer occupational preparation and wider societal needs to intellectual and personal objectives. They also feel that schools should be concerned with controversial issues and social problems rather than with more abstract aims. This egalitarian and anti-intellectualism appears further sustained through the student's perception of the schools as a right rather than a privilege, their desire to make learning fun, the material entertaining, and to ensure a less competitive learning climate. Although such changes may be termed liberal rather than conservative, the sample is apparently unlikely to look very far outside schools for any assistance in carrying out the educative process. For example, they view schools as more important for citizenship training than either the family or the community and would provide school credits for those students involved in alternative activities outside schools only if the students' activities were related to apprenticeship or on-the-job training of a vocational-technical nature.

The sample is somewhat less clear in identifying who should make decisions about the schooling process. In part, this relates to the degree of independence and the level of confidence the students evidence in their attitudes toward school administration. The ambivalence in decision making comes not so much at the classroom level where the sample is willing to listen to student concerns and assume responsibility for student learning, but at the school level where they see other factors impinging upon their responsibilities. For example, the effects of partisan politics and limited financial resources on the schools, both of which tend to explain some of the overwhelming support given to teacher unions as a lobby for teacher and student interests, were among the constraints the sample mentioned and which can be inferred to limit decentralization and teacher autonomy.

Another factor affecting the student's perceived role in decision making is a rather clear orientation toward not desiring to become involved to any appreciable extent in the administration of the school. Instead, the majority of these students expect to have an opportunity to express their opinions only regarding the institution's management. This lack of involvement, however, may not mean that the sample is against assuming more responsibility within the limits set by ministerial guidelines. Part of the problem appears to be a detachment from two-way communication with representatives of the Ministry of Education, as was apparent when 50 percent of the sample indicated that if they were to communicate some dissatisfaction to an official from the Ministry, their suggestion would not be listened to or acted upon.

Some of the lack of initiative in school administration appears to be sustained by the sample's desire to be given detailed and specific instructions in their work and only to be placed in positions in which they are certain of their abilities. The notion of dependence and lack of confidence may result as much from a prolonged dependence as students in school as it does from recognition of the fact that there exists to real expectation that school personnel should be active in making educational decisions.

Even though the students recognize their dependence on higher authorities they believe that what they do in the classroom can have an impact on their students. This influence is manifested at the individual teacher level where both a deliberate and a nondeliberate impact is believed to exist in guiding students in making career decisions. Whether or not teachers influence their students' occupational futures is perhaps less important than the fact that the sample believes that it has the potential to influence students. If these future professionals are committed to this belief, the Ministry of Education is in possession of a group of individuals who might not only make a difference in the schools but assist in reaching wider development goals through channeling secondary school graduates into careers that are deemed essential for future economic growth.

The attitude of secondary school personnel toward influencing career decisions of students would appear to interact with the sample's commitment to pursue the career for which they are being trained. Although almost all of the individuals sampled are intent on working in the secondary schools in the specific fields for which they were trained, about 30 percent would change their careers if given a second opportunity. In order to better understand this commitment and to screen out such individuals, further exploratory work with attitudinal instruments is necessary and appropriate. The implication of discovering so high a percentage of individuals who would change their careers may be a need for earlier counseling and for a more profound assessment than that provided here regarding the sample's expectations regarding the professional career they are entering.

APPENDIXES

Appendix A
Institutional Background

130. Indicate the name of the institution where you are currently enrolled.

_____

115. In what year of your university career are you enrolled?
    ____ first
    ____ second
    ____ third
    ____ fourth
    ____ fifth
    ____ other, explain: _____

116. When do you expect to graduate from this school?

_____

117. What is your major area (subject) of specialization?

_____

118. Have you completed your practice teaching?
    ____ yes
    ____ no

Appendix B
Personal Background

119. Sex:
____ male
____ female

120. Age. What month were you born? _____ What year?_____

121. Civil status:
____ single
____ married, no children
____ married, with children
____ other, please specify: _____

122. With whom are you presently living?
____ at home with parents
____ with other relatives
____ alone, or with spouse
____ with friends
____ other, please specify: _____

123. In what size city or town did you spend most of your time while growing up?
____ a town or city of more than 2,000 people
____ a town of less than 2,000 people
____ an isolated rural farm or small village

68. From a political standpoint, how would you describe yourself?
____ very liberal
____ liberal
____ moderate
____ conservative
____ very conservative
____ other: _____
____ prefer not to answer

56. What is *your* religion?

_____ none

_____ Catholic

_____ Protestant

_____ Other? Please specify: _____

Appendix C
Family Background

126. How much formal education does (did) your father have? (Check only the highest level he completed.)

_____ no formal schooling

_____ some primary schooling

_____ finished primary school

_____ some secondary schooling

_____ finished secondary school

_____ some university

_____ finished university

_____ attended graduate or professional school

127. Does your mother have a regular job outside the home?

_____ yes _____ no

128. How much formal education does (did) your mother have?

_____ no formal schooling

_____ some primary schooling

_____ finished primary school

_____ some secondary schooling

_____ finished secondary school

_____ some university

_____ finished university

_____ attended graduate or professional school

129. Were either of your parents born in a country other than Venezuela?

_____ yes _____ no

Appendix D
Student Employment

63. Have you held a job during this school year?

_____ yes

_____ no (If no, skip to question 66)

64. If yes, how many hours a week did (do) you work on this job?

_____

65. If yes, what did (do) you do in your job? _____

_____

Appendix E
Secondary School Background

37. In what year did you graduate from secondary school?_____

38. In what city is this secondary school located?_____

40. From what kind of secondary school did you graduate?
    ____ public-federal or state school
    ____ public-local school
    ____ private-Catholic school
    ____ private-other, please specify: _____

41. What type of secondary school was this?
    ____ academic   _____ agricultural
    ____ commercial   _____ technical/vocational
    ____ normal   _____ other, please specify:_____

42. What specialization did you have in secondary school?
    _____

43. About how many students were there in your secondary school graduating class?
    _____1 -10
    _____11-25
    _____26-50
    _____51-100
    _____101 or more

Appendix F
Employment Aspirations and Expectations

45. Do you plan on working in the secondary schools when you graduate from this University?

    _____ yes _____ no

47. If you *do not* plan on working in the secondary schools, what are you planning to do? _____

    _____

    _____

    _____

46. If yes, what kind of a position in the secondary school will you seek?

    _____

    _____

60. Do you think you will be a secondary school teacher five years from now?

    _____ yes

    _____ no

61. If no, what do you think you will be doing? Please specify.

    _____

69. After graduation, what subject(s) would you *prefer* to teach?

    _____

66. Upon completing your training as a teacher, in what type of school would you *prefer* to teach? (Check the kind of school, public *and/or* private)

	Public	Private
_____ academic	_____	_____
_____ commercial	_____	_____
_____ agriculture	_____	_____
_____ vocational/technical	_____	_____

	Public	Private
____ normal	____	____
____ other, please specify:	____	____

67. In what type of school do you *expect* you will be able to get a job?

_____

48. If you become a teacher, do you expect to have to earn additional income, above your teaching salary, to support yourself (and your family)?

   ____ yes

   ____ no

49. If you expect to have an additional job, what type of work do you think you will do?_____

_____

70. What is the name of the town or city where you *would like* to teach (or hold some other job) after graduation? _____

_____

71. What is the name of the town or city where you expect to work after graduation?_____

_____

Appendix G
Teachers' Unions

72. Will you join the teacher's union as soon as you get a teaching job?

    _____ yes   _____ no

58. Do you consider teachers' unions necessary?

    _____ yes   _____ no

59. If "yes," why are they necessary? (check one)

    _____ to improve conditions of work for teachers

    _____ to improve schools for children

    _____ to support teaching as a profession

    _____ other, please specify: _____

Appendix H
Teacher-Administrator Relationships

50. As a teacher, what do you expect *your* involvement will be with the administration of the school where you teach? (check one)

_____ expect to participate in policy and planning decisions

_____ expect to be consulted only regarding matters concerning me

_____ expect to be permitted to offer my opinion

_____ do not expect to actively participate in administrative affairs

51. Suppose a ruling were being considered by the Ministry of Education which you felt would be harmful to education in Venezuela. If you expressed your opinion on the ruling to an official of the Ministry, how do you think he would react? (check one)

_____ he would give your point of view serious consideration

_____ he would pay some attention to your point of view

_____ he would pay only a little attention to your point of view

_____ he would ignore what you had to say

52. If such a case arose, how likely is it that you would *actually try* to influence the ministry?

_____ very likely

_____ somewhat likely

_____ somewhat unlikely

_____ very unlikely

_____ don't know

57. Suppose you were asked to teach material which contradicted some of your own values and beliefs; what would you do?

_____ refuse to teach it or just omit it

_____ ask to have someone else teach it

_____ teach it, but give your own viewpoint

_____ try to teach it objectively, giving both sides

_____ teach it as requested, keeping your own viewpoint entirely out of it

Appendix I
Religion and Teaching

56. See Appendix B.

55. Which of the following statements best fits your present religious convections? (check one)

    _____ I do not have any religious faith

    _____ I consider myself religious, but do not take part in formal religious services

    _____ I occasionally attend religious services

    _____ I participate regularly in religious services

    _____ I am profoundly religious and always try to participate in religious activities

54. In your opinion, what importance does religious faith and belief have for the good teacher? (check one)

    _____ it is essential

    _____ it helps

    _____ it is not important

    _____ it does not help

    _____ it hinders

19. Religion should be taught in school.

    _____ Strongly Agree   _____ Agree

    _____ Strongly Disagree   _____ Disagree

Appendix J
Venezuelan Educational Needs

8. What do you feel are the *three* most critical needs of education in Venezuela today?

    1._____
    2._____
    3._____

9. If only one thing could be changed in relation to secondary schooling, what do you think it should be?

    _____
    _____
    _____

53. Which three of the following factors are *most* influential in *limiting* the quality of education in Venezuela? (check *three*)

    _____ lack of interest on the part of students
    _____ low salary level of teachers
    _____ inadequate representation of teachers in educational decision making
    _____ interference of partisan politics in educational affairs
    _____ limited economic expenditures in support of education
    _____ lack of teaching materials and facilities for efficient teaching
    _____ little cooperation from parents
    _____ large school classes and little contact between teachers and pupils
    _____ disinterest by teachers in keeping up-to-date in their teaching fields

1. It is often said that Venezuela does not have enough schools. In your opinion what *two* types of schools are most urgently needed? (Place (1) next to the type most needed and (2) next to the type second most needed.)

    _____ preschools   _____ secondary vocational/technical
    _____ primary schools   _____ university technical institutes
    _____ secondary academic   _____ university pedagogic institutes

148

_____ secondary commercial   university general preparation

_____ secondary agricultural   other, please specify:_____

_____ secondary normal   _____

_____ professional schools   _____
      (law, medicine)

Appendix K
National Development Priorities

7. What do you feel are the *three* most critical goals which Venezuela must attend to in fostering national development?

    1. _____
    2. _____
    3. _____
    _____

3. Which *two* of the following goals do you think the Venezuelan government regards as most important? (Place (1) next to your first choice, and (2) next to your second choice.)

    _____ expansion of educational opportunities

    _____ industrial development, producing more jobs

    _____ agricultural development, land reform

    _____ social and political unification

    _____ producing more high level, trained manpower

    _____ other, please specify: _____

    _____ other, please specify: _____

Appendix L
The Purposes of Education

81. Students hold a variety of Attitudes about their own educational purposes and goals. Below are descriptive statements of four such "personal philosophies" which there is reason to believe are quite prevalent. As you read the four statements, attempt to determine how close each comes to your own philosophy of education.

    PHILOSOPHY A: This philosophy emphasizes education essentially as preparation for an *occupational future*. Social or purely intellectual phases of life are relatively less important.

    PHILOSOPHY B: This philosophy, while it does not ignore career preparation, assigns greatest importance to the *scholarly pursuit of knowledge*. It attaches greatest importance to interest in ideas and to the cultivation of the intellect.

    PHILOSOPHY C: This philosophy emphasizes the *objectives and needs of the greater society*. The individual is seen as a contributor to national growth and development rather than as one who works independently for his own personal future.

    PHILOSOPHY D: This philosophy emphasizes *individualistic interests* and styles and concern for personal identity. Traditionally held value orientations or aspirations of the society at large are relatively less important.

22. Schools should emphasize the development of the intellect rather than the development of occupational skills.

    _____ Strongly Agree   _____ Agree
    _____ Strongly Disagree   _____ Disagree

84. It is more important for the schools to provide a sound academic background than to provide occupational training.

    _____ Strongly Agree   _____ Agree
    _____ Strongly Disagree   _____ Disagree

26. It is more important for schools to develop the intellect of students than to contribute to their personal identity.

_____ Strongly Agree   _____ Agree

_____ Strongly Disagree   _____ Disagree

92. The emotional and personal development of a student should be as important to a teacher as his intellectual development.

_____ Strongly Agree   _____ Agree

_____ Strongly Disagree   _____ Disagree

95. Schools should be concerned with providing individuals with the knowledge to solve pressing social problems rather than with training them for specific jobs.

_____ Strongly Agree   _____ Agree

_____ Strongly Disagree   _____ Disagree

96. Schools should teach knowledge and truth rather than being concerned with social values and norms.

_____ Strongly Agree   _____ Agree

_____ Strongly Disagree   _____ Disagree

97. Schools should be guided more by the individual interests of students than by the welfare of the society at large.

_____ Strongly Agree   _____ Agree

_____ Strongly Disagree   _____ Disagree

111. Subject matter in school should relate less to training students for jobs and relate more to the cultivation of the individual.

_____ Strongly Agree   _____ Agree

_____ Strongly Disagree   _____ Disagree

2. In your opinion, what should be the principal objectives of the school for youth 12 to 18 years of age? Indicate below the *two* which you consider most important. (Place (1) next to the most important, and (2) next to the second most important.)

_____ to prepare students for the university

_____ to develop civic responsibility

_____ to improve character

_____ to give a good general culture

_____ to prepare students for an occupation

_____ to develop reasoning capacity

_____ other, please specify: _____

82. Schools should be used to train individuals for jobs.
    _____ Strongly Agree   _____ Agree
    _____ Strongly Disagree   _____ Disagree

93. Secondary school students should be allowed to earn school credit by working in a factory or as an apprentice learning a skill.
    _____ Strongly Agree   _____ Agree
    _____ Strongly Disagree   _____ Disagree

15. Schools should emphasize student freedom, initiative, and creativity.
    _____ Strongly Agree   _____ Agree
    _____ Strongly Disagree   _____ Disagree

25. Secondary school teachers should encourage students to pursue their own individual interests.
    _____ Strongly Agree   _____ Agree
    _____ Strongly Disagree   _____ Disagree

18. Schools should permit students to establish their own individualized program of study rather than providing an established curriculum.
    _____ Strongly Agree   _____ Agree
    _____ Strongly Disagree   _____ Disagree

23. Secondary school teachers should relate the content of their courses to current social problems.
    _____ Strongly Agree   _____ Agree
    _____ Strongly Disagree   _____ Disagree

91. School is equal to life and real life problems must be emphasized in school.
    _____ Strongly Agree   _____ Agree
    _____ Strongly Disagree   _____ Disagree

27. Controversial issues should be discussed in the classroom.
    _____ Strongly Agree   _____ Agree
    _____ Strongly Disagree   _____ Disagree

89. Social values are relative to a given time and place and must be continually questioned.
    _____ Strongly Agree   _____ Agree
    _____ Strongly Disagree   _____ Disagree

83. Secondary school teachers should encourage students to question and examine social values.

_____ Strongly Agree   _____ Agree

_____ Strongly Disagree   _____ Disagree

Appendix M
The School's Relationship to Society

34. In general the overall curriculum taught in secondary school is relevant and useful to national development in Venezuela.

_____Strongly Agree   _____ Agree

_____Strongly Disagree   _____ Disagree

104. Secondary schools are providing students with the knowledge, attitudes and values which are relevant to their future lives.

_____Strongly Agree   _____ Agree

_____Strongly Disagree   _____ Disagree

101. Schools can change society by instilling appropriate attitudes and values in students.

_____Strongly Agree   _____ Agree

_____Strongly Disagree   _____ Disagree

24. Students are influenced *more* by what they learn outside of school than by what they learn in school.

_____Strongly Agree   _____ Agree

_____Strongly Disagree   _____ Disagree

33. Students who remain in school become better citizens than those who drop out of school.

_____Strongly Agree   _____ Agree

_____Strongly Disagree   _____ Disagree

85. Citizenship training should be done by the community and the family, not the school.

_____Strongly Agree   _____ Agree

_____Strongly Disagree   _____ Disagree

30. The student learns discipline for adult life by listening to adults.

_____Strongly Agree   _____ Agree

_____Strongly Disagree   _____ Disagree

102. Most Venezuelan parents are capable of teaching their children about life in a modern society.

    ____Strongly Agree   ____ Agree

    ____Strongly Disagree   ____ Disagree

36. A secondary school education is a privilege rather than a right.

    ____Strongly Agree   ____ Agree

    ____Strongly Disagree   ____ Disagree

88. As a highly educated minority, secondary school graduates have every right to expect jobs which do not require physical work.

    ____Strongly Agree   ____ Agree

    ____Strongly Disagree   ____ Disagree

109. Middle and upper class families prepare their children to achieve at a higher level in school than do lower class families.

    ____Strongly Agree   ____ Agree

    ____Strongly Disagree   ____ Disagree

35. The school is society's way of separating the rich from the poor.

    ____Strongly Agree   ____ Agree

    ____Strongly Disagree   ____ Disagree

86. Secondary schools are designed to serve the students from middle and upper class families rather than from lower class families.

    ____Strongly Agree   ____ Agree

    ____Strongly Disagree   ____ Disagree

Appendix N
School Management and Participation in Decision Making

29. A strong central government is the best way to avoid inefficiency in Venezuela's educational system.
   ____Strongly Agree   ____ Agree
   ____Strongly Disagree   ____ Disagree

98. Teachers should have considerably more to say about how schools operate.
   ____Strongly Agree   ____ Agree
   ____Strongly Disagree   ____ Disagree

57. See Appendix H

110. If controversial issues are discussed in the classroom, the teacher, as a civil servant, should be permitted to express personal opinions.
   ____Strongly Agree   ____ Agree
   ____Strongly Disagree   ____ Disagree

108. Pupils should participate in establishing the policies of a secondary school.
   ____Strongly Agree   ____ Agree
   ____Strongly Disagree   ____ Disagree

103. Secondary school teachers should invite students to help make class plans or policy.
   ____Strongly Agree   ____ Agree
   ____Strongly Disagree   ____ Disagree

21. Secondary school teachers should invite students to criticize their ideas.
   ____ Strongly Agree   ____ Agree
   ____ Strongly Disagree   ____ Disagree

90. Although many students are clamoring for new freedoms, few are capable of using those freedoms responsibly.

_____Strongly Agree   _____ Agree

_____Strongly Disagree   _____ Disagree

99. Parents should be expected to aid the school in educating their children.

_____Strongly Agree   _____ Agree

_____Strongly Disagree   _____ Disagree

107. Final decisions about education should be made by professional educators rather than by parents.

_____ Strongly Agree   _____ Agree

_____ Strongly Disagree   _____ Disagree

Appendix O
Responsibility for Student Learning

100. The teacher should decide what knowledge the child is to learn.
____ Strongly Agree   ____ Agree
____ Strongly Disagree   ____ Disagree

31. When a student fails in school, only he is to blame.
____ Strongly Agree   ____ Agree
____ Strongly Disagree   ____ Disagree

112. When a student fails in school, the teacher must accept responsibility for his failure.
____ Strongly Agree   ____ Agree
____ Strongly Disagree   ____ Disagree

106. All a teacher can do is present the material; it is up to the student to learn.
____ Strongly Agree   ____ Agree
____ Strongly Disagree   ____ Disagree

87. The classroom performance of a student should be evaluated in relation to his capacities.
____ Strongly Agree   ____ Agree
____ Strongly Disagree   ____ Disagree

32. A teacher can be effective without personally involving himself with his students.
____ Strongly Agree   ____ Agree
____ Strongly Disagree   ____ Disagree

105. It is a teacher's responsibility to help students with personal problems they may have.
____ Strongly Agree   ____ Agree
____ Strongly Disagree   ____ Disagree

20. Schools cannot be fun since students must work in order to learn anything worthwhile.

   ____ Strongly Agree   ____ Agree
   ____ Strongly Disagree   ____ Disagree

17. Secondary school teachers should try to present materials in an entertaining way.

   ____ Strongly Agree   ____ Agree
   ____ Strongly Disagree   ____ Disagree

28. Teachers should act so as to reduce the excessively competitive nature of the school system and to promote a spirit of cooperation and group effort.

   ____ Strongly Agree   ____ Agree
   ____ Strongly Disagree   ____ Disagree

94. Student freedoms should be limited in the interest of learning.

   ____ Strongly Agree   ____ Agree
   ____ Strongly Disagree   ____ Disagree

16. Without tests and grades to prod them, most students would learn little.

   ____ Strongly Agree   ____ Agree
   ____ Strongly Disagree   ____ Disagree

Appendix P
Occupational Selection

4. Why do persons usually become teachers?

    _____

    _____

    _____

6. What other factors influenced your decision to become a secondary
    school teacher? Indicate the *three* most important. (Place (1) by the
    principal factor affecting you, (2) by the second most important, and
    (3) by the third most important.)

    _____ be in control of what you do

    _____ job security

    _____ income and financial benefits

    _____ working in a satisfying environment

    _____ be treated with dignity and respect

    _____ opportunity to help others

    _____ be creative

    _____ be a professional

    _____ other, please specify: _____

113. Upon choosing your career, how much were you influenced by each of
     the following factors? (Mark one column after each of the phrases)

	Very Much	Somewhat	Not Very Much
a. Family influence or advice			
b. Professional working conditions			
c. The possibility of obtaining a high income			
d. The opportunity to learn to know yourself better			
e. The country's need for specialists in this career			
f. The influence of teachers you have known			

	Very Much	Somewhat	Not Very Much
g. Social prestige of the career			
h. Examples or influence from others you know who do the same type of work			
i. Advice or influence of freinds.			

114. Which of the reasons you indicated in the above question would you say influenced you most in the selection of your career? (Return to the previous question and mark one with a circle)

5. Which *two* people would you say influenced you the most in your decision to be a teacher? (Indicate their relationship to you by listing, for example, mother, father, uncle, elementary school teacher, secondary school classmate, etc.)

      1. _____

      2. _____

13. Do you think secondary school teachers influence their students' career choices?

      yes _____

      no _____

14. If you answered "yes" on question 13, *how* do you think teachers influence their students' career choices?

      _____

      _____

Appendix Q
Occupational Prestige

10. Please indicate your conception of the *prestige* of each of the following occupations: (check one for *each* occupation)

	Very High	High	Medium	Low	Very Low
accountant					
journalist					
baseball player					
businessman					
electrician					
large land owner					
officer in the armed forces					
high government official					
economist					
primary school teacher					
farm worker					
engineer					
movie actor					
medical doctor					
secondary school teacher					
musician					
policeman					
clergyman					
lawyer					
nurse					
nun					
university professor					
small business clerk					
soldier					
urban street cleaner					
secretary					
foreman in a factory					

	Very High	High	Medium	Low	Very Low
social worker					
scientific investigator					
farm manager					
laboratory technician					
secondary school principal					

11. From the list above, please rank the five most prestigeful occupations, by order of status. (For number one, write the most prestigeful, for number two, the second most prestigeful, etc.)

1. _____

2. _____

3. _____

4. _____

5. _____

12. Which three occupations are most important right now for the needs and growth of Venezuela?

1. _____

2. _____

3. _____

62. If you had the chance to start over again and you had sufficient means, what type of life would you prepare yourself for? (check one)

_____ an academic life (teaching, research, other scholarly work)

_____ a business life

_____ a professional life (doctor, lawyer, engineer, etc.)

_____ a life of a trained technician or craftsman

_____ a life centering upon some aspect of the creative arts

_____ I have not given sufficient thought to this matter to say

_____ other, please specify: _____

Appendix R
Work Values

73. I prefer: (check one)

_____ (a) A job where I am almost always on my own

_____ (b) A job where there is nearly always someone available to help me on problems that I don't know how to handle

74. I prefer: (check one)

_____ (a) A job where I have to make many decisions by myself

_____ (b) A job where I have to make a few decisions by myself

75. I prefer: (check one)

_____ (a) A job where my instructions are quite detailed and specific

_____ (b) A job where my instructions are very general

76. I prefer: (check one)

_____ (a) A job where I am almost always certain of my ability to perform well

_____ (b) A job where I am usually pressed to the limit of my abilities

77. I prefer: (check one)

_____ (a) A job where I am the final authority on my work

_____ (b) A job where there is nearly always a person or a procedure that will catch my mistakes

78. I prefer: (check one)

_____ (a) A job where I could be either highly successful or a complete failure

_____ (b) A job where I could never be too successful but neither could I be a complete failure

79. I prefer: (check one)

_____ (a) A job that is changing very little

_____ (b) A job that is constantly changing

80. I prefer: (check one)

    ____(a)   An exciting job but one which might be done away with in a short time

    ____(b)   A less exciting job but one which would undoubtedly exist in the company for a long time

Appendix S
Questionnaire

Instrucciones:

Este cuestionario es parte de un trabajo de investigación, preparado por dos profesores de la Universidad de California, Los Angeles, ha sido diseñado para pulsar las opiniones de los futuros profesores de educación media. El mismo es parte de un estudio en gran escala sobre profesores en Venezuela y en otras partes del mundo, y está circulando con la cooperación total del Ministerio de Educación de Venezuela y de la Dirección de esta Institución. Se le pide dar información, las razones por las cuales escogió la enseñanza como carrera, y lo que usted piensa de otras ocupaciones y de la educación en general. La información suministrada es *estrictamente confidencial.* En ningún caso se suministrará información acerca de las respuestas de un individuo en particular. Los resultados de la encuesta aparecerán como resúmenes estadísticos preparados en la UCLA y la identificación de un individuo será imposible.

Por favor, conteste libre y espontáneamente; esto no es un examen, y no hay respuestas "correctas" ni "erradas". Los resultados de este estudio servirán al Ministerio de Educación y a la Dirección de esta Institución para solucionar más efectivamente los problemas relacionados con la preparación de profesores en Venezuela.

Para llenar este cuestionario, trabaje constante y rápidamente. La mayoría de las preguntas pueden contestarse chequeando ($\sqrt{}$) una de varias alternativas. Donde se requiere información específica, trate de ser explícito, pero no gaste mucho tiempo en una sola pregunta. Si encuentra una pregunta que le confunda, por favor, contéstela lo mejor que pueda, y sírvase del margen si necesita aclarar su respuesta.

Muchas gracias por su cooperación.

Cuestionario

1. A menudo se dice que Venezuela no tiene suficientes escuelas. A su parecer, cuáles son los *dos* tipos de escuelas que se necesitan más urgentemente? (Escriba (1) junto al tipo más necesario y (2) junto al segundo).

_____ Instituciones preescolares

_____ Escuelas primarias

_____ Educación secundaria (bachillerato)

_____ Educación media comercial

_____ Educacion media agrícola

_____ Educación media normal

_____ Educacion media vocacional – técnica.

_____ Institutos técnicos universitarios.

_____ Institutos pedagógicos universitarios.

_____ Escuelas profesionales (derecho, medicina, etc.)

_____ Formación universitaria en general.

_____ otro, por favor especifique: _____

2. A su parecer, cuáles deberían ser los objetivos principales de la escuela para jóvenes de 12 a 18 años? Indique abajo los *dos* que usted considere ser los más importantes. (Escriba (1) junto al objetivo más importante y (2) junto al segundo).

_____ Preparar estudiantes para la Universidad.

_____ Desarrollar responsabilidad cívica.

_____ Mejorar el carácter.

_____ Infundirles una buena cultura general.

_____ Preparar los estudiantes para una ocupación

_____ Desarrollar la facilidad para el razonamiento

_____ otro, por favor especifique: _____

3. De las siguientes metas señale las *dos* que usted crea el gobierno venezolano considera más importantes. (Escriba (1) al lado de su primera selección, y (2) al lado de la segunda).

_____ La expansión de las oportunidades educacionales

_____ El desarrollo industrial; incrementar el número de empleos

_____ El desarrollo agrícola, la reforma agraria

_____ La unificación social y política

_____ La producción de más potencial humano de alto nivel y mejor preparación

_____ otra, por favor especifique: _____

_____ otra, por favor especifique: _____

168

4. A su juicio, cuáles cree usted que serían los motivos fundamentales para la selección de una carrera en el campo de la docencia?

_____

_____

5. Mencione *dos* personas que tuvieron mayor influencia en su decisión de hacerse profesor. (Indique cómo está relacionado con usted, escribiendo, por ejemplo: madre, padre, tío, maestro de primaria, compañero de bachillerato, etc.)

1. _____

2. _____

6. Qué otros factores influyeron en su decisión de hacerse profesor de educación media? Indique los *tres* más importantes. (Escriba (1) junto al que más le influyó, (2) junto al segundo, y (3) junto al tercero)

_____ el deseo de tener autonomía en su trabajo

_____ la estabilidad del empleo

_____ la remuneración y los beneficios sociales

_____ el deseo de trabajar en un ambiente satisfactorio

_____ el deseo de ser tratado con dignidad y respeto

_____ la oportunidad de ayudar a otros

_____ el deseo de ser creativo

_____ el deseo de ser profesional

_____ otro, por favor especifique:

7. Cuáles son las *tres* metas más críticas a las cuales debería dirigirse Venezuela para fomentar el desarrollo nacional?

1. _____

2. _____

3. _____

8. Cuáles son las *tres* necesidades más críticas de la educación venezolana hoy día?

1. _____

2. _____

3. _____

9. Si supiera que sólo una cosa relacionada con la educación media se pudiera cambiar, cuál quisiera que fuera?

_____

10. Por favor indique su concepto acerca del *prestigio* de cada una de las siguientes ocupaciones: (Marque una por *cada* ocupación).

	Muy Alto	Alto	Mediano	Bajo	Muy Bajo
Contador					
Periodista					
Jugador de béisbol					
Hombre de negocios					
Electricista					
Hacendado					
Oficial de las Fuerzas Armadas					
Alto empleado gubernamental					
Economista					
Maestro de escuela primaria					
Trabajador agrícola					
Ingeniero					
Actor					
Médico					
Profesor de educación media					
Músico					
Policía					
Sacerdote					
Abogado					
Enfermero (a)					
Monja					
Profesor universitario					
Oficinista					
Soldado					
Limpiador de calle					
Secretaria					
Capataz en una fábrica					
Trabajador social					
Investigador científico					
Caporal en una hacienda					
Técnico de laboratorio					
Director de escuela media					

11. De la lista presentada arriba, ponga en orden jerárquico las cinco ocupaciones de mayor prestigio. (Use número uno para la de más prestigio, número dos para la segunda, etc.)

1. _____

2. _____

3. _____

4. _____

5. _____

12. Cuáles son las tres ocupaciones más importantes hoy día para atender a las necesidades y el desarrollo de Venezuela?

1. _____

2. _____

3. _____

13. Piensa usted que los profesores de educación media ejercen influencia en sus alumnos en la selección de sus carreras?

Sí _____   No _____

14. Si usted contestó "sí" a la pregunta número 13, en qué manera influyen los profesores a sus alumnos en la selección de sus carreras?

_____

_____

_____

Indique el grado de acuerdo o desacuerdo que tiene usted con cada una de las siguientes afirmaciones. Por favor, dé una respuesta por cada afirmación. Es mejor anotar su primera impresión; no reflexione largo rato sobre cada frase. No hay respuestas "mejores" lo que se pide es su opinión personal. (Marque: Completamente de Acuerdo, De acuerdo, En Desacuerdo, o Completamente en Desacuerdo).

15. Las escuelas deberían poner énfasis en la libertad, iniciativa y creatividad estudiantil.

_____ Completamente de Acuerdo   _____ Completamente en Desacuerdo

_____ De Acuerdo   _____ En Desacuerdo

16. Si no tuvieran exámenes y notas que les motivara, la mayoría de los estudiantes aprendería muy poco.

_____ Completamente de Acuerdo   _____ Completamente en Desacuerdo

_____ De Acuerdo   _____ En Desacuerdo

17. Los profesores de educación media deberían tratar de presentar sus materias en forma entretenida.

_____ Completamente de Acuerdo   _____ Completamente en Desacuerdo

_____ De Acuerdo   _____ En Desacuerdo

171

18. Las escuelas deberían permitir a los estudiantes establecer sus propios programas individualizados, en vez de proporcionarles un programa preestablecido.

_____ Completamente de Acuerdo   _____ Completamente en Desacuerdo

_____ De Acuerdo   _____ En Desacuerdo

19. Se debe enseñar religión en la escuela.

_____ Completamente de Acuerdo   _____ Completamente en Desacuerdo

_____ De Acuerdo   _____ En Desacuerdo

20. Las escuelas no pueden ser agradables ya que los estudiantes, para aprender cualquier cosa valiosa, tienen que trabajar.

_____ Completamente de Acuerdo   _____ Completamente en Desacuerdo

_____ De Acuerdo   _____ En Desacuerdo

21. Los profesores de educación media deberían inducir a la crítica de sus ideas por parte de los estudiantes.

_____ Completamente de Acuerdo   _____ Completamente en Desacuerdo

_____ De Acuerdo   _____ En Desacuerdo

22. La educación debería dar más énfasis al desarrollo del intelecto que al desarrollo de las habilidades ocupacionales.

_____ Completamente de Acuerdo   _____ Completamente en Desacuerdo

_____ De Acuerdo   _____ En Desacuerdo

23. Los profesores de educación media deberían relacionar el contenido de sus cursos con problemas sociales existentes.

_____ Completamente de Acuerdo   _____ Completamente en Desacuerdo

_____ De Acuerdo   _____ En Desacuerdo

24. Lo que aprenden los estudiantes fuera de la escuela ejerce *más* influencia en ellos que lo que aprenden dentro de ella.

_____ Completamente de Acuerdo   _____ Completamente en Desacuerdo

_____ De Acuerdo   _____ En Desacuerdo

25. Los profesores de educación media deberían estimular y permitir a sus estudiantes la realización de sus intereses individuales.

_____ Completamente de Acuerdo   _____ Completamente en Desacuerdo

_____ De Acuerdo   _____ En Desacuerdo

26. Es más importante para la escuela desarrollar el intelecto de los estudiantes que contribuir al desarrollo de su personalidad.

_____ Completamente de Acuerdo   _____ Completamente en Desacuerdo

_____ De Acuerdo   _____ En Desacuerdo

27. Se deben discutir temas controversiales en el salón de clase.

_____ Completamente de Acuerdo   _____ Completamente en Desacuerdo

_____ De Acuerdo   _____ En Desacuerdo

28. Los profesores deberían tratar de reducir el carácter excesivamente competitivo del sistema escolar para promover un ambiente de cooperación y esfuerzo común.

_____ Completamente de Acuerdo   _____ Completamente en Desacuerdo

_____ De Acuerdo   _____ En Desacuerdo

29. La mejor manera de evitar la ineficiencia en un sistema educacional sería mediante una centralización educativa.

_____ Completamente de Acuerdo   _____ Completamente en Desacuerdo

_____ De Acuerdo   _____ En Desacuerdo

30. El estudiante adquiere la disciplina de su vida adulta escuchando a las personas mayores.

_____ Completamente de Acuerdo   _____ Completamente en Desacuerdo

_____ De Acuerdo   _____ En Desacuerdo

31. Si el estudiante falla en la escuela es únicamente por culpa suya.

_____ Completamente de Acuerdo   _____ Completamente en Desacuerdo

_____ De Acuerdo   _____ En Desacuerdo

32. Un profesor puede ser eficaz sin inmiscuirse en los asuntos de sus alumnos.

_____ Completamente de Acuerdo   _____ Completamente en Desacuerdo

_____ De Acuerdo   _____ En Desacuerdo

33. Los estudiantes que permanecen en la escuela llegan a ser mejores ciudadanos que aquellos que la abandonan.

_____ Completamente de Acuerdo   _____ Completamente en Desacuerdo

_____ De Acuerdo   _____ En Desacuerdo

34. En general, los programas actuales de educación media son apropiados y útiles para el desarrollo venezolano

_____ Completamente de Acuerdo   _____ Completamente en Desacuerdo

_____ De Acuerdo   _____ En Desacuerdo

35. La escuela es el vehículo mediante el cual la sociedad separa a los ricos de los pobres.

_____ Completamente de Acuerdo   _____ Completamente en Desacuerdo

_____ De Acuerdo   _____ En Desacuerdo

36. Una educación media es un privilegio y no un derecho.

_____ Completamente de Acuerdo   _____ Completamente en Desacuerdo

_____ De Acuerdo   _____ En Desacuerdo

37. En qué año egresó usted de la educación media? _____

38. En qué ciudad está situada dicha escuela? _____

39. Cómo se llama la escuela media en la cual se graduó? _____

_____

40. En qué clase de escuela media se graduó usted?

_____ Escuela media pública – nacional o estatal

_____ Escuela media pública – municipal

_____ Escuela media privada – católica

_____ otra escuela media, por favor especifique: _____

41. Qué tipo de escuela es?

_____ académica (bachillerato)   _____ técnico-vocacional

_____ comercial   _____ otro, por favor especifique:

_____ normal   _____

_____ agrícola   _____

42. Qué especialidad obtuvo usted en la escuela media?

43. Aproximadamente cuántos estudiantes se graduaron en su promoción de educación media?

_____ 1 – 10   _____ 51 – 100

_____ 11 – 25   _____ 101 o más

_____ 26 – 50

44. Si usted posee otro título de educación superior, indique su denominación.

45. Piensa usted trabajar en una escuela media cuando se gradúe en esta institución.

Sí _____   No _____

46. Si usted piensa trabajar en una escuela media, qué posición buscaría usted?

47. Si usted *no piensa* trabajar en una escuela media, qué piensa hacer?

48. Si usted se dedica a la enseñanza, además de su sueldo como docente, espera usted tener que ganar algún ingreso adicional, para sostenerse a sí mismo (y a su familia)?

Sí _____   No _____

49. Si usted espera tener que ganar algún ingreso adicional, qué tipo de trabajo piensa que haría? _____

50. Como profesor, qué tipo de relación espera tener con la dirección de la escuela donde usted enseña? (Marque uno)

_____ Espero participar en decisiones sobre política y planificación

_____ Espero ser consultado solamente en relación con los asuntos que me conciernen.

_____ Espero tener la libertad de expresar mi opinión.

_____ No espero participar activamente en asuntos administrativos.

51. Suponga que el Ministerio de Educación estuviera considerando una decisión que usted piensa haría daño a la educación venezolana. Si usted expresara su opinión acerca de ella a un funcionario calificado del Ministerio, cómo piensa que él reaccionaría? (Marque uno)

_____ El consideraría seriamente su punto de vista.

_____ El prestaría alguna atención a su punto de vista.

_____ El prestaría poca atención a su punto de vista.

_____ El ignoraría totalmente lo que usted le diría.

52. Si tal caso se presentara, cuán probable sería que usted *realmente tratara* de influir en el Ministerio?

_____ Muy probable

_____ Posible

_____ Improbable

_____ Muy improbable

_____ No sé

53. Seleccione entre los siguientes factores los *tres* que usted considera limitan, en parte, la calidad de la educación venezolana? (Marque tres)

_____ La falta de interés por parte de los estudiantes

_____ El bajo nivel de sueldo de los profesores.

_____ La representación inadecuada de los profesores en el proceso de decisiones educacionales.

_____ La intervención de la política partidista en asuntos educativos.

_____ Los limitados recursos económicos asignados en favor de la educación.

_____ Falta de materiales y facilidades para una enseñanza eficaz.

_____ La poca cooperación de los padres y representantes de los alumnos.

_____ El gran número de alumnos por aula y el escaso contacto entre profesores y alumnos.

_____ El poco interés que muestran los profesores en mantenerse al día en sus especialidades educativas.

54. A su parecer, qué importancia tienen para un buen profesor su fe y creencia religiosas? (Marque uno)

_____ Son esenciales   _____ No ayudan

_____ Ellas ayudan   _____ Son obstáculos

_____ No son importantes

175

55. Cuál de las siguientes afirmaciones describe mejor sus presentes convicciones religiosas? (Marque uno)

_____ No tengo ninguna creencia religiosa

_____ Me considero religioso, pero no participo en servicios religiosos formales.

_____ Asisto, ocasionalmente, a servicios religiosos

_____ Participo regularmente en servicios religiosos.

_____ Soy profundamente religioso y siempre trato de participar en actividades religiosas.

56. Cuál es su religión?

_____ Ninguna

_____ Católica

_____ Protestante

_____ otra, por favor, especifique: _____

57. Suponga que se le pidiera enseñar material que contradijera algunos de sus propios valores y creencias, qué haría usted? (Marque uno)

_____ Me negaría a enseñarlo, o simplemente lo omitiría

_____ Pediría a otra persona que lo enseñara.

_____ Lo enseñaría, pero presentaría mi propio punto de vista.

_____ Trataría de enseñarlo objetivamente, presentando los puntos alternativos.

_____ Lo enseñaría tal como me fuera solicitado, excluyendo mi propio punto de vista.

58. Considera usted necesarias las Asociaciones de Profesores?

_____ Sí   _____ No

59. Si usted contestó afirmativamente a la pregunta número 58, por qué son necesarias las asociaciones de profesores? (Marque uno)

_____ Para mejorar las condiciones del trabajo de los profesores

_____ Para mejorar la enseñanza

_____ Para defender la docencia como profesión

_____ otra, por favor especifique: _____

_____

60. Piensa usted que continuará siendo profesor en ejercicio de educación media dentro de cinco años?

_____ Sí   _____ No

61. Si usted contestó negativamente a la pregunta número 60, qué piensa usted estar haciendo? Por favor especifique. _____

_____

62. Si usted tuviera la oportunidad de empezar de nuevo y tuviera los medios suficientes, para qué tipo de trabajo se prepararía? (Marque uno)

_____ Un trabajo académico (enseñanza, investigación, etc.)

_____ Un trabajo en los negocios

_____ Una carrera profesional (médico, abogado, ingeniero, etc.)

_____ Un trabajo técnico o artesanal

_____ Un trabajo enfocando algún aspecto de las artes creativas

_____ No he pensado suficientemente este asunto.

_____ otro, por favor especifique:

63. Ha tenido usted un empleo durante este año escolar?

_____ Sí   _____ No

(Si su respuesta es negativa, pase a la pregunta número 66)

64. Si usted contestó afirmativamente a la pregunta número 63, cuántas horas por semana trabajó (o está trabajando) en este empleo?

_____

65. Si trabajó (o está trabajando) este año, qué tipo de labores estuvo (está) desarrollando? Por favor especifique: _____

_____

_____

66. Al terminar su preparación de profesor, en qué tipo de escuela *preferiría* enseñar? (Indique la clase de escuela, pública y/o privada)

	Pública	Privada
_____ Académica (bachillerato)		
_____ Comercial		
_____ Agrícola		
_____ Técnico-vocacional		
_____ Normal		
_____ otra, por favor especifique:		

67. En qué tipo de escuela espera usted poder conseguir un empleo? Por favor especifique: _____

68. Desde el punto de vista político, cómo se describiría usted a sí mismo? (Marque uno)

_____ Extrema izquierda

_____ Izquierda

_____ Moderado

_____ Derecha

_____ Extrema derecha

_____ otro, por favor especifique: _____

_____ Prefiero no contestar

69. Después de su graduación, qué materia (s) *preferiría* enseñar?

_____

_____

177

70. Ha pensado en la ciudad o el pueblo donde le gustaría enseñar (o desempeñar algún otro empleo) después de su graduación? Indique el nombre de ese lugar.

_____

71. Cómo se llama la ciudad o el pueblo donde usted *espera* trabajar después de su graduación?

_____

72. Se hará miembro de la Asociación de Profesores?

_____ Sí _____ No _____ No lo he pensado.

73. Prefiero: (Marque uno)

_____ Un trabajo casi a mi entera responsabilidad.

_____ Un trabajo en el cual casi siempre tendría alguien disponible para ayudarme a resolver problemas.

74. Prefiero: (Marque uno)

_____ Un trabajo en el cual yo tenga que tomar muchas decisiones por mi cuenta.

_____ Un trabajo en el cual yo tenga que tomar pocas decisiones.

75. Prefiero: (Marque uno)

_____ Un trabajo en el cual mis instrucciones sean bastante específicas y detalladas.

_____ Un trabajo en el cual mis instrucciones sean muy generales.

76. Prefiero: (Marque uno)

_____ Un trabajo en el que esté casi siempre seguro de mis habilidades para desempeñarlo bien.

_____ Un trabajo en el que esté generalmente bajo presión hasta el máximo de mis habilidades.

77. Prefiero: (Marque uno)

_____ Un trabajo en el cual yo tenga la decisión final en lo que concierne a mi trabajo.

_____ Un trabajo donde yo siempre tenga una persona o un procedimiento que descubra mis errores.

78. Prefiero: (Marque uno)

_____ Un trabajo donde pueda tener indistintamente éxito o fracaso completo.

_____ Un trabajo en el cual nunca pueda tener completo éxito o fracaso.

79. Prefiero: (Marque uno)

_____ Un trabajo que cambia muy poco

_____ Un trabajo que cambia constantemente

80. Prefiero: (Marque uno)

_____ Un trabajo estimulante, pero que podría cesar en cualquier momento.

_____ Un trabajo menos estimulante, pero que, indudablemente, permanecería más estable.

81. Los estudiantes apoyan variadas actitudes acerca de sus propios metas y propósitos educativos. A continuación se presentan descripciones de cuatro de tales filosofías personales. A medida que lea estas descripciones trate de determinar cuan parecida es cada una de ellas a su propia filosofía educativa.

Filosofía A: Esta filosofía pone énfasis en la educación esencialmente como preparación para un *futuro ocupacional.* Las fases sociales o puramente intelectuales de la vida son relativamente menos importantes.

Filosofía B: Esta filosofía, aunque no ignora la preparación ocupacional, asigna mayor importancia a la *búsqueda intelectual del conocimiento.* Ella pone el mayor énfasis en el interes por las ideas y en el cultivo del intelecto.

Filosofía C: Esta filosofía pone énfasis en los *objetivos y necesidades de la sociedad.* Se ve al individuo más como un ente que contribuye al crecimiento y desarrollo nacional que como un ser que trabaja independientemente por su propio futuro personal.

Filosofía D: Esta filosofía pone énfasis en los *intereses individuales* y se preocupa por la identidad personal. Las orientaciones o aspiraciones de los valores tradicionalmente mantenidas por la sociedad en general, son relativamente menos importantes.

Evalúe jerárquicamente la precisión con que cada filosofía refleja *su* propio punto de vista (Escriba (1) al lado de la filosofía que *mejor* describa su punto de vista, (2) al lado de la que siga, luego (3) y (4) al lado de aquellas que menos se ajustan a sus apreciaciones de estas materias).

_____ Filosofía A

_____ Filosofía B

_____ Filosofía C

_____ Filosofía D

Indique el grado de acuerdo o desacuerdo que tiene usted con cada una de las siguientes afirmaciones. Por favor dé una respuesta por *cada* afirmación. Es mejor suministrar su primera impresión; no piense largo rato sobre cada frase. No hay respuestas "mejores" lo que se pide es su opinión personal. (Marque Completamente de Acuerdo, De Acuerdo, En Desacuerdo o Completamente en Desacuerdo).

82. Los profesores de educación media deberían estimular a los estudiantes a para el trabajo.

_____ Completamente de Acuerdo   _____ Completamente en Desacuerdo

_____ De Acuerdo   _____ En Desacuerdo

83. Los profesores de educación media debería estimular a los estudiantes a examinar y cuestionar los valores sociales.

_____ Completamente de Acuerdo   _____ Completamente en Desacuerdo

_____ De Acuerdo   _____ En Desacuerdo

84. Es más importante que las escuelas proporcionen sólidos conocimientos académicos que enseñanza ocupacional.

_____ Completamente de Acuerdo   _____ Completamente en Desacuerdo

_____ De Acuerdo   _____ En Desacuerdo

85. La enseñanza cívica debería ser proporcionada por la communidad y la familia, no por la escuela.

_____ Completamente de Acuerdo   _____ Completamente en Desacuerdo

_____ De Acuerdo   _____ En Desacuerdo

86. Las escuelas medias sirven a los estudiantes de las familias de clase media y alta en vez de a estudiantes de clase baja.

_____ Completamente de Acuerdo   _____ Completamente en Desacuerdo

_____ De Acuerdo   _____ En Desacuerdo

87. La actuación de un alumno en el aula debería ser evaluada en relación a sus capacidades.

_____ Completamente de Acuerdo   _____ Completamente en Desacuerdo

_____ De Acuerdo   _____ En Desacuerdo

88. Los egresados de la escuela media tienen el derecho a esperar empleos que no requieran trabajo físico en razón a su preparación.

_____ Completamente de Acuerdo   _____ Completamente en Desacuerdo

_____ De Acuerdo   _____ En Desacuerdo

89. Los valores sociales están ligados a un tiempo y un espacio específicos y tienen que ser cuestionados contínuamente.

_____ Completamente de Acuerdo   _____ Completamente en Desacuerdo

_____ De Acuerdo   _____ En Desacuerdo

90. A pesar de que muchos estudiantes están pidiendo más libertades, pocos son capaces de usarlas responsablemente.

_____ Completamente de Acuerdo   _____ Completamente en Desacuerdo

_____ De Acuerdo   _____ En Desacuerdo

91. La escuela es representativa del mundo externo y por lo tanto los problemas cotidianos deben ser acentuados en ella.

_____ Completamente de Acuerdo   _____ Completamente en Desacuerdo

_____ De Acuerdo   _____ En Desacuerdo

92. El desarrollo personal y emocional de un estudiante debería ser tan importante para un profesor como su desarrollo intelectual.

_____ Completamente de Acuerdo   _____ Completamente en Desacuerdo

_____ De Acuerdo   _____ En Desacuerdo

93. Debería permitirse a los estudiantes de media obtener créditos escolares por el trabajo efectuado en una fábrica o como aprendices de algún oficio.

_____ Completamente de Acuerdo   _____ Completamente en Desacuerdo

_____ De Acuerdo   _____ En Desacuerdo

94. Las libertades estudiantiles deberían ser limitadas en el interés de la enseñanza.

_____ Completamente de Acuerdo   _____ Completamente en Desacuerdo

_____ De Acuerdo   _____ En Desacuerdo

95. Las escuelas deberían preocuparse por suministrar a los estudiantes el conocimiento necesario para resolver problemas sociales urgentes, en vez de prepararlos para empleos específicos.

_____ Completamente de Acuerdo   _____ Completamente en Desacuerdo

_____ De Acuerdo   _____ En Desacuerdo

96. Las escuelas deberían comunicar el conocimiento y la verdad, en vez de preocuparse por los valores y normas sociales.

_____ Completamente de Acuerdo   _____ Completamente en Desacuerdo

_____ De Acuerdo   _____ En Desacuerdo

97. Las escuelas deberían ser guiadas más por los intereses individuales de los estudiantes que por el bienestar de la sociedad en general.

_____ Completamente de Acuerdo   _____ Completamente en Desacuerdo

_____ De Acuerdo   _____ En Desacuerdo

98. Los profesores deberían ser consultados más a menudo acerca del funcionamiento de la escuela.

_____ Completamente de Acuerdo   _____ Completamente en Desacuerdo

_____ De Acuerdo   _____ En Desacuerdo

99. Debería esperarse que los padres ayuden a la escuela en el proceso de educar a sus hijos.

_____ Completamente de Acuerdo   _____ Completamente en Desacuerdo

_____ De Acuerdo   _____ En Desacuerdo

100. El profesor debería decidir cuáles conocimientos debe aprender el estudiante.

_____ Completamente de Acuerdo   _____ Completamente en Desacuerdo

_____ De Acuerdo   _____ En Desacuerdo

101. Las escuelas pueden cambiar la sociedad inspirando en los estudiantes los valores y actitudes apropiados.

_____ Completamente de Acuerdo   _____ Completamente en Desacuerdo

_____ De Acuerdo   _____ En Desacuerdo

102. La mayoría de los padres venezolanos son capaces de enseñar a sus hijos lo que deben saber acerca de la vida en una sociedad moderna.

_____ Completamente de Acuerdo   _____ Completamente en Desacuerdo

_____ De Acuerdo   _____ En Desacuerdo

103. Los profesores de media deberían solicitar la ayuda de los estudiantes en la preparación de sus planes y programas de sus clases.

_____ Completamente de Acuerdo   _____ Completamente en Desacuerdo

_____ De Acuerdo   _____ En Desacuerdo

181

104. Las escuelas medias proporcionan a los estudiantes conocimientos, actitudes y valores apropiados para su vida futura.

_____ Completamente de Acuerdo   _____ Completamente en Desacuerdo

_____ De Acuerdo   _____ En Desacuerdo

105. Es la responsabilidad de un profesor ayudar a los estudiantes en la resolución de los problemas personales que puedan tener.

_____ Completamente de Acuerdo   _____ Completamente en Desacuerdo

_____ De Acuerdo   _____ En Desacuerdo

106. Todo lo que puede hacer el profesor es presentar el material de clase; aprenderlo es la responsabilidad del estudiante.

_____ Completamente de Acuerdo   _____ Completamente en Desacuerdo

_____ De Acuerdo   _____ En Desacuerdo

107. Las decisiones finales acerca de la educación deberían ser tomadas por los educadores profesionales y no por los padres.

_____ Completamente de Acuerdo   _____ Completamente en Desacuerdo

_____ De Acuerdo   _____ En Desacuerdo

108. Los estudiantes deberían participar en el establecimiento de las políticas de la escuela media.

_____ Completamente de Acuerdo   _____ Completamente en Desacuerdo

_____ De Acuerdo   _____ En Desacuerdo

109. Las familias de las clases media y alta preparan a sus hijos para que se destaquen mejor en las actividades escolares que los hijos de familias de la clase baja.

_____ Completamente de Acuerdo   _____ Completamente en Desacuerdo.

_____ De Acuerdo   _____ En Desacuerdo

110. En el caso de que asuntos controversiales sean discutidos en el aula, debería permitírsele al profesor, como servidor de la sociedad, expresar sus opiniones personales.

_____ Completamente de Acuerdo   _____ Completamente en Desacuerdo

_____ De Acuerdo   _____ En Desacuerdo

111. La materia enseñada en las escuelas debería referirse menos a la preparación de los estudiantes para el trabajo y más cultivo del individuo.

_____ Completamente de Acuerdo   _____ Completamente en Desacuerdo

_____ De Acuerdo   _____ En Desacuerdo

112. El Profesor debe aceptar la responsabilidad si sus estudiantes fallan.

_____ Completamente de Acuerdo   _____ Completamente en Desacuerdo

_____ De Acuerdo   _____ En Desacuerdo

113. Al escoger su carrera, qué importancia tuvo para usted cada uno de los siguientes puntos? (Marque una columna después de cada punto).

	Muy Import.	Algo Import.	Sin Import.
a. Consejo, influencia o tradición familiar			
b. Condiciones de trabajo profesional			
c. La posibilidad de obtener altos ingresos			
d. Aprender a conocerse mejor			
e. La necesidad en el país de especialistas en esta carrera			
f. Influencia de maestros que conocía			
g. Prestigio social de la carrera			
h. Ejemplo o influencia de conocidos que hacen la misma clase de trabajo			
i. Consejo o influencia de amigos			

114. Cuál de las razones indicadas en la pregunta anterior considera que influyó más en la elección de su carrera? (Vuelva a la pregunta anterior y marque una sola con un círculo).

115. En qué año de su carrera universitaria está usted inscrito? (Marque uno)

_____ Primero

_____ Segundo

_____ Tercero

_____ Cuarto

_____ Quinto

_____ Otro, por favor especifique:

116. Cuándo espera graduarse en esta institución?_____
_____

117. Cuál es su especialidad dentro de su carrera? _____
_____

118. Ha completado usted su práctica docente?

_____ Sí   _____ No

119. Sexo:

_____ Masculino   _____ Femenino

120. Edad:

En qué mes nació usted? _____ En qué año? _____

183

121. Estado Civil:

_____ Soltero

_____ Casado, sin hijos

_____ Casado, con hijos

_____ otro, por favor especifique: _____

122. Con quién vive usted actualmente?

_____ en casa, con sus padres

_____ con otros familiares

_____ solo, o con su cónyuge

_____ con amigos

_____ otro, por favor especifique:_____

123. Cuál es el tamaño de la ciudad o el pueblo donde usted vivió la mayor parte de su niñez.

_____ una ciudad o un pueblo de más de 2.000 habitantes

_____ un pueblo de menos de 2.000 habitantes

_____ Una hacienda rural o un caserío aislado

124. Cuál es la ocupación de su padre? (Si su padre está jubilado o muerto, indique su ocupación pasada)

_____

125. Describa en una o dos frases la ocupación de su padre. Trate de dar una idea clara de lo que hace (o hacía). Por ejemplo, si es un obrero o un empleado público o un hombre de negocios, etc. díga lo que hace en la fábrica, oficina, o negocio en que trabaja; si es un hombre de negocios díga también en qué tipo de empresa trabaja; si es un profesor o maestro, díga en qué tipo de escuela o institución enseña primaria, secundaria, o superior, etc.

_____

_____

_____

126. Qué nivel de educación formal alcanzó su padre? (Indique solamente el más alto nivel)

_____ ninguna educación formal

_____ alguna educación primaria

_____ terminó la educación primaria

_____ alguna educación media

_____ terminó la educación media

_____ alguna educación universitaria

_____ terminó la educación universitaria

_____ siguió cursos de post-grado

127. Trabaja su madre regularmente fuera de la casa.

_____ Sí   _____ No

128. Qué nivel de educación formal alcanzó su madre? (Indique solamente el más alto nivel)

_____ ninguna educación formal

_____ alguna educación primaria

_____ terminó la educación primaria

_____ alguna educación secundaria

_____ terminó la educación secundaria

_____ alguna educación universitaria

_____ terminó la educación universitaria

_____ se graduó en una escuela profesional (por ejemplo, derecho, medicina o siguió cursos de post-grado).

129. Nació alguno de sus padres fuera de Venezuela?

_____ Sí   _____ No

130. Indique el nombre de la institución en la cual está matriculado.

_____

185

Appendix T
Factor Analysis of the
Research Instrument

Included in the survey questionnaire was a set of fifty-three "agree-disagree" statements (questions 15-36, 82-112) designed to sample the attitudes of respondents regarding the educational process and the purpose of education. While these items were drawn independently from a variety of sources it was anticipated that the content of the items had a high degree of association. In an attempt to verify the statistical validity of this assumption, factor analysis was employed to look for clustering within the range of variables in order to establish the statistical heterogeneity of the data.

As the principal use of these data was to provide descriptions of respondent attitudes, it is important that those abstract qualities which we refer to as attitudes be identified as precisely as possible. In most survey reports such as this, attitudes are described from the content of the question which measures them, rather than by describing the universe (factor) of which the individual question was merely an expression. Factor analysis is useful for analyzing the internal structure of many intercorrelated variables such as those included here, and detecting dimensions of commonality. Positive results will permit the reduction of the body of test variables to fewer, more meaningful dimensions.[1]

Variables

The fifty-three questionnaire attitude items tested for association were responded to on a four point Likert-type continuous scale. Quantitative values from 4 (agreement) to 1 provide mean scores for this analysis.

The fifty-three variables were selected because they represented specified dimensions or "factors" which are presumed to describe

[1]I wish to thank Roger Riske, a student in the Graduate School of Education, UCLA, for his assistance with this analysis.

separate domains of educational activity. This presumption derives from explications of educational theory and the work of other researchers. From the selection criteria and an intuitive evaluation of the items it was speculated that eight disparate domains might be represented by these items: (1) the purpose of schooling, (2) teacher role, (3) student freedom and initiative, (4) administrative decision making, (5) school and curriculum reform, (6) parental involvement, (7) political influences, and (8) the impact of school upon individuals and society.

Assumptions and Delimitations

This research has assumed that attitudes are differentially formed and are randomly distributed, and that they are measurable, with statistical consistency, by means of the scaling technique employed in the questionnaire. It has also been assumed that the respondent cases represent a normal distribution.

Analytical Model

Data from the 623 cases was used for the analysis. The data were factor analyzed looking for principal component commonality and an orthogonal matrix was used to indicate the cumulative portion of variance accounted for by each basic factor. A cut-off point accounting for the majority of present variance, and also reducing the factors to a more manageable number, was accomplished. Verimax rotation was then performed to identify the factor loadings. Factor interpretation and identification was used to permit the appropriate conclusions to be drawn. A second analysis was then performed to examine the influence of principal axis commonality in an attempt to identify only the specific variance common to the correlation matrix.

Results

I. Conducting a principal component factor analysis we determined that 60 percent of the total variance in the correlation matrix would be accounted for by fifteen factors. We then rotated (orthogonal) the principal fifteen factors and analyzed the proportion of variance (r^2) accounted for in each factor. The arbitrary point below which we rejected variables as input into a

187

factor was .40. We also arbitrarily rejected any factor that had fewer than four variables contributing significantly ($\geq$ 0.40) to it. Results are as follows:

Factor 1 included items 24, 30, 31, 32, 33, 34, 36, 37, 39, 40, 41, 42, 44, 45, 46, 47, 48, 51, 52, 53.

Factor 2 included items 1, 3, 4, 7.

Factor 3 included items 2, 16, 19, 20.

Factor 4* included items 21, 22, 27.

Factor 5* included items 12, 25.

Factor 6* included items 8, 25, 36.

Factor 7* included items 13, 35, 49.

Factor 8* included item 18.

Factor 9* included item 17.

Factor 10* included items 28, 29, 30.

Factor 11* included items 23, 24, 26.

Factor 12* included item 6.

Factor 13 included items 9, 10, 11, 13.

Factor 14* included items 38, 43.

Factor 15* included no items.

*Factor not analyzed because of less than four items contributing to the factor.

The model is thus reduced to factors 1, 2, 3, and 13, comprising half of the total test items: 1, 2, 3, 4, 7, 10, 11, 13, 16, 19, 20, 31, 33, 34, 36, 37, 39, 40, 42, 44, 45, 46, 47, 49, 51, 53.

II. In the principal axis factor analysis, specific variance and error are eliminated using a correlation coefficient that takes into account only common variance. Eigenvalues by the principal axis method include a number of negative figures. As only the positive eigenvalues were used in computing the cumulative proportion of total variance, only 43 percent of the total variance was accounted for by using the twenty-nine variables yielding a positive eigenvalue. Rotating fifteen factors again, we analyzed the variables using the same cut-off point of $r = 0.40$, below which we would not retain an item. Again, factor 1 had by far the most variables with high correlation coefficients.

Results are as follows:

Factor 1 included items 24, 31-34, 36, 39-42, 44-49, and 51-53.

Factor 2 included items 1, 3, 4, 7.

The rest of the factors that were comprised of items with significant correlation coefficients (≥ 0.40) had loadings with fewer than four items:

Factor 3 included items 8, 25.

Factor 4 included items 2, 16.

Factor 6 included items 21, 22.

Factor 10 included item 24.

Factor 12 included item 11.

Factor 14 included item 49.

Comparing the two results, we note that the item loading for factor 1 is about the same in both tests, and that for factor 2 is exactly the same. Thereafter, however, the factors are comprised of fewer than four items that have an $r \geq 0.40$ and the variables are not at all the same as in the first test.

Analysis and Interpretation

Looking at the variables that have an r^2 relationship with factor 1, we note that the items tested refer to a broad area of inquiry with little seeming homogeneity. There is little statistically identifiable intervariable commonality, but, rather, the range of attitudinal items seems to represent disparate qualitative contexts. In factor 2, the grouping of items can be partially identified as relating to the subject of "teacher presentation and student contributions." That is, a seeming factor represented by items 1, 3, 4, and 7 regarding the teachers' reception to change from traditional presentation, openness to criticism, and student input to the schooling process, including curriculum (refer to the specific items in the questionnaire).

Factor 3 seemingly pertains to "student classroom department" reflecting students' attitudes toward externally imposed discipline and its effects on scholastic and extrascholastic behavior.

189

Factor 13 seems to relate to educational "relevance" (the included items referred to the applicability of school content to social problems and the need for and desirability of learning outside the classroom). -

Conclusions

The first factor, however amorphous it may be, includes fifteen or so items that are highly correlated. Factor 1 accounted for 60 percent of the total variance of these attitude items. The wide distribution of test items which was observed and the relatively low intercorrelation values suggest, however, that the questionnaire asks such a broad range of questions that it would be highly speculative to reduce the fifty-three separate items into fewer common factors.

As the instrument was not fully pretested some questions remain as to what is being measured. The questions seem unambiguous and to be designed to elicit relevant attitudinal measures. In a visual comparison of item correlation coefficients some of the items that should seemingly have had high intercorrelation did not, further indicating the distinct quality of each attitude item.[2]

---

[2]While one could also question the internal reliability of the measuring instrument from those results, the low correlation might not be an indication of low reliability for two reasons. First, respondents could have perceived statements appearing to be dichotomous merely as being two of many alternatives. To use an example items 17 and 53 (17: "When a student fails in school only he is to blame;" 53: "When a student fails in school the teacher must accept responsibility for his failure") respondents could exonerate both the teacher and the child when failure results. Thus, although the intent of the questions is to force the respondent to choose between placing the blame on one of the two, he may have thought that extraneous forces beyond the control of either was culpable. Second, although the correlation was low, the variation was such that in most questions we were unable, owing to variance approaching or exceeding 1.0, to accurately determine whether or not certain students holding strongly to one issue were also more likely to feel the same way about any other given issue. Indeed, criticisms of the statistical technique and test methodology which are well known to measurement experts account for a fair degree of ambiguity in these results. The important conclusion is, however, that items reported here do seem to be representing independent and separate data and not one facet of a longer homogeneous dimension. The questionnaire items are used herein in a manner consistent with this conclusion.

190

Bibliography

Albornoz, Orlando. *El Maestro y la Educación en la Sociedad Venezolana.* Caracas, 1965.

América en Cifras, 1970 Situación Cultural: Educación y Otros Aspectos Culturales. Washington, D.C.: Organización de los Estados Americanos, Instituto Interamericano de Estadística, 1971.

Averch, Harvey A., et al. *How Effective Is Schooling? A Critical Review and Synthesis of Research Findings.* Santa Monica, Calif.: Rand Corporation, 1972.

Babladelis, George, and Suzanne Adams. *The Shaping of Personality.* Englewood Cliffs, N.J.: Prentice Hall, 1967.

Bell, Wendell, Richard J. Hill, and Charles R. Wright. *Public Leadership.* San Francisco: Chandler, 1961.

Bendix, Reinhard, and S. M. Lipset. *Class, Status, and Power: A Reader in Social Stratification,* rev. ed. New York: Free Press, 1966.

Bernbaum, G., et al. "Intra-Occupational Prestige Differentiation in Teaching," *Pedagógica Europea.* London: W. & R. Chambers, 1969.

Bloom, Benjamin. *Stability and Change in Human Characteristics.* New York: John Wiley, 1964.

Blum, Albert A., ed. *Teachers Unions and Associations: A Comparative Study.* Urbana, Ill.: University of Illinois Press, 1969.

Bonilla, Frank. *The Failure of Elites.* Cambridge, Mass.: Massachusetts Institute of Technology Press, 1970.

Central Advisory Council on Education. *Children and Their Primary Schools.* London: Her Majesty's Stationery Office, 1966.

Cicourel, Aaron V., and John I. Kitsuse. *The Educational Decision Makers.* New York: Bobbs-Merrill, 1963.

Coleman, James S., et al. *Equality of Educational Opportunity.* Washington, D.C.: U.S. Government Printing Office, 1966.

191

Collins, Randall. "Functional and Conflict Theories of Educational Stratification," *American Sociological Review,* 36 (1971), 1002-1019.

Coombs, Philip H. *The World Educational Crisis.* New York: Oxford Press, 1968.

Davies, Margarita. *Survey of the Status of the Teaching Profession in the Americas.* Washington, D.C.: World Confederation of Organizations of the Teaching Profession, 1964.

Departamento de Investigaciones Educacionales. *Estadísticas Educacionales.* Dirección de Planeamiento, Ministerio de Educación, Cuadro 8, Página 237, Caracas, Venezuela: 1971.

Etzioni, Amatai. *The Semi-Professions and Their Organization.* New York: Free Press, 1969.

Evans, David R. *Teachers as Agents of National Development: A Case Study of Uganda.* New York: Praeger (Special Studies), 1971.

Federación Venezolana de Maestros, Mérida, Venezuela: Universidad de los Andes, 1966.

Flanders, Ned A. *Teacher Influence, Pupil Attitudes, and Achievement.* Washington, D.C.: U.S. Office of Education, 1965.

Foster, Philip. *Education and Social Change in Ghana.* London: Routledge and Kegan Paul, 1965.

Gross, Neal, Noel F. McGinn, David Napior, and Walter O. Jewell, III. "Planning for Educational Change: An Application of Sociological and Psychological Perspectives." Cambridge, Mass.: Center for Studies in Education and Development, Harvard University, August 5, 1968 (typewritten copy).

Hansen, Mark. *Educational Reform in Colombia and Venezuela: An Organizational Analysis.* Occasional Papers in Education and Development, no. 4. Cambridge, Mass.: Center for Studies in Education and Development, Harvard University, August 1970.

Havighurst, Robert J., and Aparecida Gouveia. *Brazilian Secondary Education and Socio-Economic Development.* Praeger Special Studies in International Economics and Development. New York: Praeger, 1969.

Hoyle, Eric. "Professional Stratification and Anomie in the Teaching Profession," *Pedagogica Europea.* London: W. & R. Chambers, 1969.

Illich, Ivan. *Deschooling Society.* New York: Harper and Row, 1970.

Instituto Pedagógico Experimental Informe Anual, 1968-69. Barquisimeto, julio de 1969.

Instituto Pedagógico Experimental. "Bases Organizativas," Barquisimeto, Estado Lara, Venezuela, n.d.

Jahoda, Marie, and Neil Warren, eds. *Attitudes*. Baltimore, Md.: Penguin, 1966.

Katz, Llihu, and Paul F. Lazarsfeld. *Personal Influence: The Part Played by People in the Flow of Mass Communications*. New York: Free Press, 1955.

Kunkel, John. *Society and Economic Growth*. New York: Oxford Press, 1970.

Lipset, Seymour Martin. "Values, Education, and Entrepreneurship," in Seymour Martin Lipset, and Aldo Solari, eds. *Elites in Latin America*. New York: Oxford University Press, 1967. Pp. 3-60.

Lipset, Seymour M., and Aldo Solari, eds. *Elites in Latin America*. New York: Oxford, 1967.

Matrícula del Instituto Pedagógico de Caracas Discriminada por Entidades Federales y Otras Nacionalidades. El Pedagógico en Cifras, Boletín del Servicio de Estadística, no. 4. Año Lectivo 1967-1968, Caracas, Venezuela, Pedagogic Institute, n.d.

Más y Mejor Educación, Análisis Estadístico, Ministerio de Educación, Dirección de Planeamiento. Caracas, Venezuela, 1969.

Más y Mejor Educación, Añalysis Estadístico, Ministerio de Educación, Dirección de Planeamiento, Caracas, Venezuela, 1970.

McClelland, David. *The Achieving Society*. Princeton, N.J., D. Van Nostrand, 1961.

Memoria y Cuenta, 1971, que el Ministro de Educación presenta al Congreso Nacional de la República de Venezuela en sus sesiones de 1972. Tomo I y Tomo II, Depto. de Publicaciones, Imprenta del Ministerio de Educación.

Morrison, A., and D. McIntyre. *Teachers and Teaching*. Baltimore, Md.: Penguin, 1969.

Musgrove, Frank, and Philip H. Taylor. *Society and the Teacher's Role*. London: Routledge and Kegan Paul, 1969.

Nam, Charles B., and John K. Folger. *Education of the American Population*. Washington, D.C.: U.S. Bureau of the Census, 1967.

Organization of Economic Cooperation and Development. *Development of Secondary Education: Trends and Implications*. Paris, France: Organization of Economic Cooperation and Development, 1969.

193

Parsons, Talcott. *Essays in Sociological Theory, Pure and Applied.* Glencoe, Ill.: Free Press, 1949.

_____. *The Social System.* Glencoe, Ill.: Free Press, 1951.

Revenga, José Rafael. "The Efficacy of Education in Venezuela." Paper presented to the Conference on Venezuela: Panorama, 1969, John Hopkins University, November 10-11, 1969.

_____. *Education in Venezuela: A 1936-1970 Overview.* 1970.

Rosenfeld, Howard, and Alvin Zander. "The Influence of Teachers on Aspirations of Students," *Journal of Educational Psychology,* 52 (Feb. 1961), 1-11.

Rostow, Walt W. "The Take-off into Self-sustained Growth," *Economic Journal,* 66 (March 1956), 25-48.

Ruscoe, Gordon C. "Individual Decisions and Educational Planning: Occupational Choices of Venezuelan Secondary Students," *International Development Review,* 10 (June 1968), 20-25.

Sánchez, George I. *The Development of Education in Venezuela.* U.S. Dept. of Health, Education and Welfare, Washington, D.C.: OE-14086, Bulletin no. 7, 1963.

Schultz, Theodore W. *The Economic Value of Education.* New York: Columbia University Press, 1963.

Seeman, Melvin. *Social Status and Leadership: The Case of the School Executive.* Columbus, Ohio: Ohio State University, 1960.

Smith, B. Othaniel. *Research in Teacher Education.* Englewood Cliffs, N.J.: Prentice-Hall, 1971.

"The Changing Role of the Teacher," *Educational Technology,* 10 (February, 1970), entire issue.

Thorsten Husein. "Does More Time in School Make a Difference?" *Saturday Review,* April 29, 1972, pp. 32-35.

UNESCO Statistical Yearbook. Paris, France: UNESCO, 1970.

U.S. Office of Education. *Do Teachers Make a Difference? A Report on Recent Research on Pupil Achievement.* Washington, D.C.: U.S. Office of Education, 1970.

Williams, Lawrence K. "Development of a Risk-Taking Scale." Unpublished working paper, School of Industrial Relations, Cornell University, 1962.